56

Angels
ON ASSIGNMENT

PERRY STONE

Charisma
HOUSE
A STRANG COMPANY

ANGELS ON ASSIGNMENT by Perry Stone
Published by Charisma House
A Strang Company
600 Rinehart Road
Lake Mary, Florida 32746
www.strangbookgroup.com

Design Director: Bill Johnson
Cover design by Justin Evans

Library of Congress Cataloging-in-Publication Data:
Stone, Perry F.
  Angels on assignment / by Perry Stone. -- 1st ed.
      p. cm.
  ISBN 978-1-59979-752-6
 1. Angels--Christianity. 2. Intercessory prayer--Christianity. 3.
Spiritual warfare. 4. Mizpah (Israel) I. Title.
  BT966.3.S75 2009
  235'.3--dc22

                                    2009027563

This publication has been translated in Spanish under the title *Angeles en misión*, copyright © 2009 by Perry Stone, published by Casa Creación, a Strang company. All rights reserved.

10 11 12 13 14 — 10 9 8 7 6 5 4
Printed in the United States of America

Contents

Introduction

ESCAPE FROM DEATH

DURING MORE THAN FIFTY YEARS OF LIVING, MY LIFE has been miraculously spared on several occasions. In 1961, I was sitting in the front seat of Dad's 1960 Comet automobile when my father topped a hill, smashing into another car that was stopped on the road without its brake lights working. The impact sent my mother into the windshield, caused my father to bend the steering wheel around the steering column, and caused me to smash into the metal dashboard. My mother, who had injuries of a broken jaw and knee, saw my limp body under the dashboard amid broken glass and was gripped with fear. She suspected that I had broken my neck. Then suddenly she was overjoyed to hear me crying. The sounds broke her chilly fear of death, especially when she realized that I was just sobbing because my shoe had been knocked off my foot by the impact.

Years later in 1966, our family of five survived another accident when late one night my mother fell asleep while driving and crossed over the yellow line, heading toward a head-on collision with an oncoming eighteen-wheeler. I was asleep in the back and awoke with the car skidding, jerking sideways, and abruptly stopping on the side of a hill. A tree, acting like a roadblock, prevented the car from flipping over on the mountain. The trucker said, "I saw your car coming toward me and reached for an emergency flare, knowing you were going to smash into me head-on; however, something picked your car up and set it over on the hill." He suggested, quite correctly, that someone above was watching over us.

I learned later that it was the intercessory prayer of my father that prevented the possible tragedy of our family's death that night. Twelve hours before the accident, we had been in Ohio at my aunt Janet's house. Early that morning, Dad was in the bedroom groaning and travailing in prayer because he sensed that some form of danger was coming that day. The close call came twelve hours later that night. Yet, by sunrise we were back in the same car and headed home to Big Stone Gap, Virginia.

A few years ago, I was flying in the right seat of the cockpit of the ministry's 421 twin-engine plane with my friend and pilot, Kevin Wright. At thirteen thousand feet in the air, and about twenty minutes from landing in Chattanooga, Tennessee, the plane suddenly veered to the left, and I heard a sound similar to a car engine that misfires when water is mixed with the fuel. A few seconds later it occurred again, and I watched a piston monitor in front of me reveal that the right engine went out. We had lost an engine in midair! Time froze for a few seconds as the pilot put in an emergency call to the air control in Atlanta. After receiving advice, we chose to fly on one engine into Chattanooga, landing the limping plane at a few minutes after midnight.

After landing, I told the pilot that I strongly sensed that someone was praying for us at that very moment. After he returned home, his wife said, "Are you OK?"

He replied, "I am now."

She asked, "What happened?"

As he told the story, his wife, Denise, commented, "The Lord put a burden on me, and I haven't ceased to pray for you since I saw you leave church early to pick Perry up in Kentucky. I was burdened from that moment and prayed continually because I felt you were in some type of trouble."

The following day I telephoned our head prayer leader, Bea Ogle, who directs fifteen hundred intercessors who pray for our ministry. I asked her how she was doing, and she said she was fine. However, she informed me that the night before, she had felt impressed at 11:00 p.m. that I was in some type of danger and prayed without ceasing until about 12:15 a.m. Our engine failure happened a little after 11:00 p.m., and we landed shortly after 12:15 a.m.! It was the intercessory prayers of Denise and Bea that sustained us in the plane that night.

Over the years, whenever my dad's spirit was overwhelmed with a burden, he would enter into deep, travailing prayer. It was always proven later that he had interceded against some form of danger, either in the family or linked with someone we knew. Intercessory prayer and learning to follow a prayer burden has spared my life and our family members' lives on several occasions.

> THE MIZPAH COVENANT WILL RELEASE THE ASSISTANCE OF ANGELS AND WILL FORGE A PROTECTIVE COVENANT AROUND YOU AND YOUR LOVED ONES.

In this book I will teach you the importance of prayer and intercession to prevent attacks of the enemy. But there is more to this book. I want to teach you about a unique, seldom-taught *covenant* that asks God to release angels to assist you, and forges a protective covenant around your companion, your children, and you.

This covenant, called the Mizpah covenant, is one of the most unusual covenants in Scripture and is related to God's protection when two people are away from one another. Join me in a wonderful, in-depth study of the Word on a subject that I never heard taught when I was growing up in the church. However, I have personally experienced this covenant blessing, and I want to teach you about it so you also can experience it.

—PERRY STONE

Chapter 1

LIVING IN THE SHADOW OF THE ALMIGHTY

> Be merciful unto me, O God, be merciful unto
> me: for my soul trusteth in thee: yea, in the
> shadow of thy wings will I make my refuge,
> until these calamities be overpast.
>
> —PSALM 57:1, KJV

THE TIME IS IN THE LATE 1970s. IMAGINE THAT YOU have an eighteen-year-old son whose work assignment consists of traveling from state to state by automobile. At times he must drive ten to fifteen hours one way, through major cities such as Atlanta, Birmingham, and even New York City. To arrive in time for some prearranged engagements, he must literally leave at ten o'clock at night and drive all night to make it to the next meeting. He travels alone.

At that time there were no cell phones, BlackBerry devices, iPhones, text messaging, or GPS systems—only printed maps and pay phones at convenience stores. At times you expect him home from an all-night trip by eight o'clock in the morning, but he arrives hours later. During these times you wonder if he's in danger. Did he have a flat tire, engine trouble, or could he have run out of gas on a long country road in the mountains of West Virginia? It's just that parental nature to be *concerned*.

Who is that young, eighteen-year-old lad? That boy is me. I was called into the ministry at age sixteen, and by age eighteen, I began traveling throughout five different states, driving at all hours of the night to get from one church to another. My father, Fred Stone, once had wavy, jet-black hair. His hair turned silver, and he always said, "Perry, this white hair was a result of me staying up all hours of the night and praying for your safety and protection when you were traveling across the nation." Having a teenage son myself now, I can confirm the same feelings of my father.

DANGER SURROUNDS US

Life is like a long path with unknown sections of quicksand and pits along the way. When a mother sends her son, or a wife her husband, to a battlefield in a foreign land, her heart skips a beat each time a twenty-four-hour cable newscast interrupts programming to show a bombing or a suicide attack in the same area where her soldier son or husband is stationed. Children have been sent to public schools in the morning never to return home in the evening because of evil seducers and perverse-minded adults who took advantage of their innocence. The unexpected even occurs on college campuses when a mentally unstable student turns a gun on colleagues out of anger or hate. Shift work divides the quality time in families, requiring a wife or husband to travel to a factory late at night, often through dangerous parts of the city.

In reality, we need continual protection—at home, on the job, on the road, and basically twenty-four hours a day.

There are numerous scriptures indicating that God *can* and *will* protect us. One of the common English words that indicates God's protective plan is the word *keep*. When the ancient Jewish high priest spoke the priestly blessing over the people, he would say, "The LORD bless thee, and keep thee" (Num. 6:24, KJV). The Hebrew word for keep is *shamar*, and it means to hedge in, guard, and protect. One of the greatest Scripture passages, and one of my personal favorites, is Psalm 91. I call it the psalm of divine protection:

> He who dwells in the secret place of the Most High
> Shall abide under the shadow of the Almighty.
> I will say of the LORD, "He is my refuge and my fortress;
> My God, in Him I will trust."
>
> Surely He shall deliver you from the snare of the fowler
> And from the perilous pestilence.
> He shall cover you with His feathers,
> And under His wings you shall take refuge;
> His truth shall be your shield and buckler.
> You shall not be afraid of the terror by night,
> Nor of the arrow that flies by day,
> Nor of the pestilence that walks in darkness,
> Nor of the destruction that lays waste at noonday.
>
> A thousand may fall at your side,
> And ten thousand at your right hand;
> But it shall not come near you.
> Only with your eyes shall you look,
> And see the reward of the wicked.

Because you have made the LORD, who is my refuge,
Even the Most High, your dwelling place,
No evil shall befall you,
Nor shall any plague come near your dwelling;
For He shall give His angels charge over you,
To keep you in all your ways.
In their hands they shall bear you up,
Lest you dash your foot against a stone.
You shall tread upon the lion and the cobra,
The young lion and the serpent you shall trample
    underfoot.

"Because he has set his love upon Me, therefore I will
    deliver him;
I will set him on high, because he has known My name.
He shall call upon Me, and I will answer him;
I will be with him in trouble;
I will deliver him and honor him.
With long life I will satisfy him,
And show him My salvation."

—PSALM 91:1–16

This powerful passage begins in the very first verse with four different Hebrew names for God:

- The Most High—*El Elyon*
- The Almighty—*El Shaddai*
- The Lord—*YHVH*
- My God—*El*

These four Hebrew names reveal the total sum of what God is and what He can be in a person's life. He is the covenant-keeping God (*YHVH*), the provider of all of our needs (*El*

Shaddai), the only God (*El Elyon*), and the strong One (*El*). The writer of this psalm, believed to be Moses, is revealing the names of God that were revealed in the first five books of the Bible, called the Torah. In fact, from the time of Adam to the time of Moses, God had only revealed certain names to His people. After Moses went to Egypt, God revealed a new name to Moses that the Hebrews had never heard:

> And God spake unto Moses, and said unto him, I am the LORD: and I appeared unto Abraham, unto Isaac, and unto Jacob, by the name of God Almighty, but by my name JEHOVAH was I not known to them.
>
> —EXODUS 6:2–3, KJV

This name that the English Bible spells Jehovah in Hebrew is actually a four-letter name called the tetragrammaton (meaning four-letter word) and is identified as the sacred name of God. It is spelled with four Hebrew letters: *yod, hei, vav,* and *hei* (*YHVH*). This name is translated in the Old Testament English translation 6,823 times as "Lord" and "Lord God." This name is considered so sacred that eventually only the high priest was permitted to speak it. Today in a synagogue, when the biblical scrolls are read and speakers come to this four-letter name, they will not attempt to speak it because the name is sacred and they do not know the actual pronunciation, but they will replace it by saying, "Adonai," another name for God.

In Psalm 91, Moses speaks about the "secret place of the Most High" and about abiding "under the shadow of the Almighty." For many years I was uncertain as to the meaning of the "secret place" and the "shadow of the Almighty." After speaking to rabbis in Jerusalem and doing much research,

I believe I can share some interesting insights.

In Moses's time, the "secret place" was the holy of holies in the tabernacle of Moses. It was secret in that only the high priest was permitted to enter the chamber once a year, on the Day of Atonement, to make atonement for sins (Lev. 16:23, 27–28). It was strictly forbidden for any other person to pass beyond the large handwoven veil that separated the holy place from the most holy place. The holy of holies housed the sacred ark of the covenant, the golden box that stored a golden pot of manna, the rod of Aaron, and the tablets of the Law, and was the secret place of God.

THE SHADOW OF THE ALMIGHTY

The meaning of the "shadow of the Almighty" requires a more detailed study. There are five passages, including Psalm 91, that mention the shadow of God's wings. Four of the five are listed below:

> Keep me as the apple of the eye, hide me under the shadow of thy wings.
>
> —PSALM 17:8, KJV

> How excellent is thy lovingkindness, O God! Therefore the children of men put their trust under the shadow of thy wings.
>
> —PSALM 36:7, KJV

> Be merciful unto me, O God, be merciful unto me: for my soul trusteth in thee: yea, in the shadow of thy wings will I make my refuge, until these calamities be overpast.
>
> —PSALM 57:1, KJV

> Because thou hast been my help, therefore in the shadow
> of thy wings will I rejoice.
>
> —Psalm 63:7, kjv

To understand the shadow of God's wings, we must go back to the time of David. Moses and his builders constructed a large tent made of wooden beams and animal skins, called a *tabernacle*, and pitched it in the wilderness for almost forty years. (See Exodus 26.) After Joshua possessed the Promised Land, the tent was pitched in Israel in the area of Shiloh (1 Sam. 1–3). Hundreds of years after Joshua, David desired that God's presence dwell in Jerusalem, thus he personally had the ark of the covenant transferred from the tabernacle of Moses to the city of Jerusalem (2 Sam. 6). David prepared a special tent to house the ark of the covenant, initiating twenty-four-hour, nonstop worship, singing, and praying within the tent. This special tent is named the tabernacle of David.

> David built houses for himself in the City of David; and he prepared a place for the ark of God, and pitched a tent for it.
>
> —1 Chronicles 15:1

> So they brought the ark of God, and set it in the midst of the tabernacle that David had erected for it. Then they offered burnt offerings and peace offerings before God.
>
> —1 Chronicles 16:1

Not only did the golden ark rest in Jerusalem in David's tent, but also the king organized and appointed numerous musicians and singers to minister before the ark, including scribes to be *recorders* and to write down the inspired utterances that would be spoken as people worshiped near the ark:

> And he appointed certain of the Levites to minister before the ark of the LORD, and to record, and to thank and praise the LORD God of Israel: Asaph the chief, and next to him Zechariah, Jeiel, and Shemiramoth, and Jehiel, and Mattithiah, and Eliab, and Benaiah, and Obed-edom: and Jeiel with psalteries and with harps; but Asaph made a sound with cymbals; Benaiah also and Jahaziel the priests with trumpets continually before the ark of the covenant of God.
>
> —1 CHRONICLES 16:4–6, KJV

After researching details related to the ark of the covenant and learning of David's tent, I understood that the *shadow of God* mystery was linked to the ark and somehow understood by David in relation to the tabernacle he built for the sacred article.

The ark was a box constructed of acacia wood, covered within and without with pure gold. There was a heavy lid of solid gold called the "mercy seat" and two golden cherubim, beaten from sheets of gold, placed on the mercy seat with their wings overshadowing the mercy seat and their faces looking downward (Exod. 25:10–22).

David's tabernacle differed from Moses's sacred tent. Moses's tabernacle had three sacred chambers: the outer and inner courts and the holy of holies. The holy of holies was the room that held the ark of the covenant. In Moses's tabernacle, only the high priest was permitted to enter the holy of holies once a year on the Day of Atonement in order to sprinkle blood on the mercy seat of the ark. In David's tent, however, worshipers were permitted to stand near the ark and worship.

The only *wings* linked to God's presence are the wings of the cherubim sitting on the mercy seat of the ark. How would these wings become a *shadow of God*?

In 1988 I talked with a Canadian rabbi in Jerusalem, giving him my theory of the "shadow of the Almighty." More than likely, the tent of David would have been a large square or perhaps rectangle tent made of animal skins, similar to Moses's tabernacle. The ark would have sat on a level surface of white limestone rock, which is the type of rock under the hills in and around Jerusalem. The tent would have a covering to prevent the natural elements from harming the ark. In warm, sunny weather, the covering could be rolled back and the light of the sun would cast light on the wings of the golden cherubim on the mercy seat, forming a shadow on the ground. This would become the "shadow of the Almighty" and the "shadow of His wings." David knew that only the Levites could physically touch or move the ark of the covenant. However, while in worship within the tabernacle a person could kneel in the shadow of the ark when its reflection was cast on the floor by the light of the sun. When I expressed these theories to the rabbi, he replied that my concept would have been correct.

The inspired writer of the four passages in Psalms understood that once he or anyone else could get into the shadow of God's presence, there was unlimited protection from the human and spiritual conflicts that surrounded them. If we were to compare this physical activity of being in the shadow of God to our time, we would say today that these individuals had *intimate time* in the presence of the Lord through worship or prayer.

The ark of the covenant no longer sits in Moses's tabernacle, David's tent, or Solomon's temple. Whether it was lost over time, stolen by invading armies, or hidden under the Temple Mount, men may never really know. However, the purpose of the ark was to provide a picture of the future atonement through the Messiah.

From the time of Moses, there were three sacred items stored within the golden box of the ark of the covenant. They were a golden pot of the manna, the stone tablets of the Law of God, and the rod of Aaron, which had blossomed and produced almonds (Heb. 9:4). Each item was a prophetic picture of a spiritual blessing that would be imparted to believers under the new covenant. Christ said He was the "bread which came down from heaven" (John 6:41, KJV); thus, the manna in the wilderness that sustained the nation was a preview of the living bread that would bring the gift of eternal life to all who would partake of His body and blood (John 6:53–58). After conversion, a person learns to live by the Word of God. Christ said man lives by "every word that proceeds from the mouth of God" (Matt. 4:4). The tablets of the Law in the ark of the covenant were the Law (or Word) of God written on stone. Once we are saved by grace, we must learn from the Word. The third item in the ark was the rod of Aaron. This dead tree branch in the hands of the man of God was the

> JUST AS THE ROD OF AARON BLOSSOMED AND PRODUCED FRUIT, A BELIEVER WHO RECEIVES THE HOLY SPIRIT WILL ALSO PRODUCE SPIRITUAL FRUIT IN HIS OR HER LIFE.

instrument used to produce miracles (Exod. 7:12). The rod was a picture of the power of the Holy Spirit, which would abide in the believer.

The ark that rested on the stone floor in the holy of holies is a picture of Christ Himself. He is the living manna, the Word made flesh (John 1:14), who sent the Holy Spirit with His nine gifts and nine fruit to inhabit your body, the temple of the Holy Spirit. Just as the rod of Aaron blossomed and produced fruit, a believer who receives the Holy Spirit will also produce spiritual fruit in his or her life (John 15:2–8).

We receive and enjoy our spiritual blessings when we enter the presence of God. However, our blessings often come with battles, and our battles often precede spiritual breakthroughs. Thus, there is a mystery associated with why the righteous suffer and with the purpose of struggles, conflicts, and battles in our life.

Chapter 2

WHEN BAD THINGS HAPPEN TO GOOD PEOPLE

So went Satan forth from the presence of the LORD, and smote Job with sore boils from the sole of his foot unto his crown.

—JOB 2:7, KJV

ONE OF LIFE'S MOST PERPLEXING MYSTERIES IS WHY BAD things happen to good people. We have all heard the stories of how the most dedicated teenager in the church was suddenly killed in an automobile accident, or how the beautiful young mother with three children is stricken with cancer and suddenly passes, leaving her infants to be raised by loving family members. Why the righteous suffer has always been an enigma.

Jesus told us that it would "rain on the just and on the unjust" (Matt. 5:45, KJV). This statement alludes to the fact that storms come to both righteous people and those who are unrighteous. Job said, "Man who is born of woman is of few days and full of trouble," and "Man is born to trouble, as the sparks fly upward" (Job 14:1; 5:7).

Preventing Bad Things

There is no one set reason or explanation as to why bad things happen. However, after years of ministry, I have some observations as to what may, at times, help *prevent* bad things from occurring:

1. Avoid making wrong choices.

A shortcut through a dangerous part of a city at night is not a wise choice. Leaving your wallet or purse on the seat of your car while you stop at a convenience store for a restroom break is foolish. Mowing the grass on a riding mower on a steep hill could get you killed and has injured and taken the lives of several individuals I personally knew. Seat belts are not placed in automobiles to admire when you take your seat. The barrel of a gun is not a small telescope to look through, and driving drunk can lead to your name being on the funeral home marquee. When people make unwise choices, they can open the door to difficulty or tragedy.

2. Don't override better judgment.

Years ago a noted pastor with a church of a thousand members was ministering in Kentucky. He desired to return to Ohio on Saturday night to be present for his regular Sunday morning service. He and his two sons were returning in a small plane. The weather was very bad, and several individuals warned him not to make the trip because it was too dangerous. He overrode his better judgment and the warning signs, and shortly after takeoff, the plan crashed into the trees. *His personal desire overruled his better judgment.* When numerous individuals advise us not to do something, it is wise to pay attention since "in a multitude of counselors there is safety" (Prov. 24:6).

3. Do your job properly.

Years ago, my wife, Pam, and I were enjoying Sunday dinner at the Holiday Inn in Cleveland, Tennessee, with one of our spiritual sons, a convert named Wayne McDaniel. After dinner, I drove off in my van and he in his. I took a road heading left, and he continued straight. Within five minutes I heard the fire trucks and the ambulances roaring past us in the direction we had come. I told Pam, "I didn't see an accident; where are they going?" Thirty minutes later I received a call that the brakes on Wayne's van had gone out, and he had lost control of his van, flipping it over a guardrail and landing among trees. About forty-eight hours later, he passed away in the intensive care unit.

Driving to the hospital, I remembered a brief statement he had made a few days prior. He said, "My brakes are going bad; I need to get them fixed. They feel like they may go out." He either forgot or didn't take the time to fix the problem. Bad brakes are like a loose electrical wire in a house—something bad could happen if they are not repaired or fixed. Wayne's accident reminded me of a scripture in Ecclesiastes 7:17 (AMP):

> [Although all have sinned] be not wicked overmuch or willfully, neither be foolish—why should you die before your time?

I could spend more time listing the reasons why bad things can happen. However, I would prefer to share how we can prevent bad things from happening. Without question, if you and I were not protected in some manner by the hand of God, we would have already stepped into eternity. My life has been spared from death in car accidents on three occasions. Was it by chance? No, it was by prayer.

4. Don't be in the wrong place with the wrong people at the wrong time.

Whomever you rub shoulders with will rub off on you. Many teens find themselves in dangerous, life-threatening situations, especially with drugs and alcohol, because their friends, like magnets, are pulling them into sin. Many teens have been with the wrong people in the wrong place at the wrong time and suffered a terrible consequence, including premature death. Solomon wrote, "If sinners entice you, do not consent" (Prov. 1:10).

All of the above examples were the results of people not paying attention, not listening, or not following wisdom. There are many times in life that circumstances occur over which we have no control. For example, I have friends who were cashing a check in a local bank when suddenly an armed robber entered the facility waving a firearm and screaming to everyone to get on the floor. Others were hit broadside when a careless driver darted through a red light. The homes of believers have been leveled to piles of firewood when hurricanes blew apart their dwelling, peeling walls off the wooden frames as if they were mere toothpicks. In these and countless other examples, believers feel helpless to defend themselves or their families. For this reason, we need to know and understand God's ability, willingness, and promises to protect His people.

A COVENANT OF PROTECTION

There are numerous covenants in Scripture that were ratified with just one person, yet the impact of those covenants is still felt today.

God made a covenant agreement with Noah after the universal Flood that He would never destroy the planet with water again (Gen. 9:13–15). As a permanent sign for all mankind, God placed the rainbow in the sky. Each time it rains while the sun is shining, the reflection forms a beautiful, multicolored rainbow that more than four thousand years later still reminds humanity of the *token* of God's promise to Noah and future generations.

> THE MIZPAH COVENANT IS A PROMISE OF GOD'S ABILITY, WILLINGNESS, AND PROMISE TO PROTECT HIS PEOPLE.

Another covenant was forged with Abraham. God promised Abraham's children, the Jews, that they would inherit the land of Israel forever (Gen. 13:15). Following nineteen hundred years of dispersion, Israel was reborn as a nation in 1948, and the natural seed of Abraham, the Jewish people, have returned from the four regions of the earth to their original homeland.

For many years I have taught on the covenants of the Bible, emphasizing the new covenant that was ratified by the blood of Christ. After many years of reading and researching the Scripture, I observed that there was one covenant made between a father-in-law and his son-in-law that I knew existed in the Old Testament, but I had never identified it as a pattern for a practical covenant for believers until doing detailed research. It is called the *Mizpah covenant.*

Chapter 3

MIZPAH—FORGING A COVENANT OF PROTECTION

> So Jacob took a stone and set it up as a pillar. And
> Laban said, "This heap is a witness between you
> and me this day." Therefore its name was called
> Galeed, also Mizpah, because he said, "May the
> LORD watch between you and me when we
> are absent one from another. If you afflict my
> daughters, or if you take other wives besides
> my daughters, although no man is with us—see,
> God is witness between you and me!"
>
> —GENESIS 31:45, 48—50

PERHAPS YOU THINK YOUR FAMILY OR A FAMILY YOU know has some dysfunctional genes hidden in the DNA that occasionally flow in the bloodline of a few relatives. If so, then you have something in common with ancient peoples of the Bible. Growing up, we were amazed by the many stories from the Scriptures. As a child, I often visualized these biblical families as such holy, flawless people to whom no one living today could even hold a candle. Then as I got older and read the *rest of the story*, I realized the extreme fallibility of so many who loved God in their hearts but fell short in their walks.

THE ORIGINAL DYSFUNCTIONAL FAMILIES

Take Noah for example. Noah was the hero of the Flood. He took a hundred years to build a floating zoo and saved himself and seven members of his family from drowning in the murky water. I guess that after the Flood, Noah decided that one hundred fifty days of being cooped up with smelly animals was too much, so he planted a vineyard, got drunk, took his clothes off, and ended up placing a curse on his grandson Canaan (Gen. 9:20–27).

Lot was considered a righteous man (2 Pet. 2:7–8). However, when the Sodomites in the city attempted to tear the door down to "get to know" two strangers (men who were actually angels) in Lot's house, he offered his two daughters to the perverted gang of twisted men. Later, after running from the burning city, he too became drunk and had relations with his daughters, who birthed two sons through their own father (Gen. 19:35–38).

Then there was Samson. He couldn't resist Delilah's *haircutting salon* and kept paying a visit to the Philistines who lived on the *other side of the tracks*. Eventually, Delilah put scissors to Samson's hair, breaking his Nazirite vow and costing him his anointing, his eyesight, and his strength (Judg. 16:6–28). Samson could rip gates from city walls, tie three hundred foxes' tails together, and use a donkey's jawbone to slay a thousand Philistines, but seduction from one good-looking woman did more damage than a thousand Philistines.

We all know David the lion-, bear-, and giant-killer, but what about David the voyeur? He was on his roof scoping out a woman taking a bath. This was not just any woman; it was the wife of one of David's mighty men named Uriah. The king eventually had an affair, the woman became pregnant with David's child, and David had the husband killed in a battle to hide his own sin (2 Sam. 11). It is amazing to consider that David had strength to kill a bear, lion, and giant but became weak when a beautiful woman crossed his path.

THE ORIGINAL FUGITIVE

The stories go on. Our attention is now focused on Jacob the son of Isaac. Rebekah, Isaac's wife, conceived twin sons as opposite as the north and south poles. Esau was a hunter, a smelly outdoorsman whose arms were covered with thick, red hair. His brother, Jacob, was a mama's boy who seemed to enjoy hanging around the kitchen. Being the firstborn, Esau was given both the birthright and the blessing (Gen. 27:36).

> AS GOD'S COVENANT PEOPLE, THERE IS A COVENANT OF PROTECTION THAT CAN LINK GOD'S ANGELIC PROTECTION TO YOUR LIFE AND THE LIVES OF YOUR LOVED ONES.

During a moment of hunger and weakness, Esau sold his birthright to Jacob for a bowl of lentils (Gen. 25:30–34). Years later, Jacob tricked his nearly blind father into praying the impartation blessing over him instead of his older brother, Esau. In the days of the patriarchs, the father's blessing was considered the final act before he passed on. The prophetic blessing the father spoke over the sons usually came to pass, for their words were marked by the family and honored by the Lord.

When Esau discovered that his younger brother, Jacob, had disrupted the divine order and received Isaac's blessing, more than his arms were red! No doubt his blood pressure shot through the roof, and fire was in his eyes. Rebekah instructed her son Jacob to leave home for *a few days* and to go to her brother Laban's house in Syria until Esau's anger cooled down (Gen. 27:44). Mama never knew those few days would turn into twenty years before Jacob returned home.

THE BLESSING FOLLOWED JACOB

As far as material wealth, it appears that Jacob left home with little or nothing and ended up in Syria at his uncle Laban's estate. Business began picking up when Jacob saw Rachel, one of Laban's two daughters. It was love at first sight, and Jacob agreed to work seven years for her hand in marriage. After seven years of hard labor, the joke was on Jacob, and he got a taste of his own medicine because Laban had tricked him. Instead of giving Jacob his daughter Rachel, Laban gave him Leah (Gen. 29:25).

A week later, Laban gave Rachel to Jacob, but with the agreement that Jacob would work for him seven more years. Although Jacob's wages were changed ten times and he worked in the cold and heat for twenty years, God prospered him because of the spoken blessing his father had placed on him twenty years earlier (Gen. 31:7). Laban knew God's special blessing and favor was upon his son-in-law, Jacob.

TIME TO MAKE A BREAK FROM "DADDY"

After twenty years, Jacob knew it was time to return to the Promised Land. Secretly, Jacob took his two wives, Rachel and Leah, their eleven sons, the handmaidens, servants, and a huge herd of animals and left Laban's estate in Syria to return with this large entourage to his homeland.

Days later, Laban was told that Jacob, his daughters, his grandkids, and the animals were missing. He took a group of servants and went after Jacob with the intent of harming him. God appeared to the angry father and father-in-law in a dream and warned him not to speak good or evil of Jacob:

> And Laban was told on the third day that Jacob had fled. Then he took his brethren with him and pursued him for seven days' journey, and he overtook him in the mountains of Gilead. But God had come to Laban the Syrian in a dream by night, and said to him, "Be careful that you speak to Jacob neither good nor bad."
> —GENESIS 31:22–24

This warning may have saved Jacob's life. When any father believes his daughter is being abused, mistreated, or threatened, the cat becomes a lion, and the persons doing harm had better get out of Dodge or be prepared for the wrath of a protective dad. Laban made haste and pursued Jacob, catching up with the entire group:

> So Laban overtook Jacob. Now Jacob had pitched his tent in the mountains, and Laban with his brethren pitched in the mountains of Gilead. And Laban said to Jacob: "What have you done, that you have stolen away

unknown to me, and carried away my daughters like captives taken with the sword? Why did you flee away secretly, and steal away from me, and not tell me; for I might have sent you away with joy and songs, with timbrel and harp? And you did not allow me to kiss my sons and my daughters. Now you have done foolishly in so doing."

—Genesis 31:25–28

Dads Love Their Little Girls

It may be difficult to understand Laban's feelings of anger and distress unless we slip the shoes on our own feet. Imagine having your son-in-law working as a leading CEO in your business, creating massive amounts of prosperity, raising eleven of your grandchildren, and suddenly you wake up to learn he has taken your daughters, the grandchildren, and a portion of your wealth to a neighboring country! A young man leaving home is one thing, but when the daddy of two girls is involved, the wrath of a father rises like the boiling lava from a volcanic eruption.

It was in this setting that a unique covenant was forged between Laban and Jacob. It is this covenant of protection that is one of the most fascinating studies, linking God's angelic protection for His covenant people.

Chapter 4

MIZPAH AND THE ANGEL OF THE COVENANT

Then Laban said to Jacob, "Here is this heap and here is this pillar, which I have placed between you and me. This heap is a witness, and this pillar is a witness, that I will not pass beyond this heap to you, and you will not pass beyond this heap and this pillar to me, for harm. The God of Abraham, the God of Nahor, and the God of their father judge between us." And Jacob swore by the Fear of his father Isaac.

—GENESIS 31:51–53

THE HEBREW WORD FOR COVENANT IS *B'RITH*, WHICH alludes to a cutting to forge an agreement between two parties. Throughout the Old Testament, the numerous covenants that are recorded involved some form of a blood offering, a sacrifice, or a covenant meal to seal the deal.

- Noah built an altar after the Flood and offered a sacrifice (Gen. 8:20).

- Abraham built an altar and offered a sacrifice (Gen. 12:7).
- Jacob built altars and offered sacrifices (Gen. 35:6–7).
- David built an altar to stop a plague (2 Sam. 24:25).

Laban was concerned for the security and safety of his two daughters. He knew Jacob tended to be a trickster and had a conniving personality. In the early Canaanite culture, it was common for one man to have numerous wives. Laban entered a covenant with Jacob and told him that the Lord would be watching him and his daughters when they were apart. He warned Jacob not to mistreat his two daughters and not to marry any other woman.

Covenants were often established at an altar, or an altar was built following a covenant, so a sacrifice could follow. When Laban and Jacob entered a covenant with one another, there is no record of an altar being built, but there was a large *pile of stones* (called a heap) where they ate and a large stone pillar erected as a permanent marker and memorial. The pillar became a boundary between Jacob and Laban.

Jacob followed through with a normal procedure when a covenant was ratified:

> Then Jacob offered a sacrifice on the mountain, and called his brethren to eat bread. And they ate bread and stayed all night on the mountain.
>
> —Genesis 31:54

This agreement between a father-in-law and his son-in-law reveals all of the important features that were a part of ancient Hebrew covenants:

1. The agreement is made between the two parties.
2. A blood sacrifice is made upon an altar.
3. A special covenant meal is eaten.
4. An altar, stone monument, or pillar is erected as a memorial.

The stone heap became a "witness," or a visible testimony between Jacob and his future generations and Laban's future descendants. It was established so that neither group would do harm to the other.

> And Laban said, "This heap is a witness between you and me this day." Therefore its name was called Galeed, also Mizpah, because he said, "May the LORD watch between you and me when we are absent one from another."
>
> —GENESIS 31:48–49

Laban's estate in Syria was a long way from Jacob's home in Canaan. There were no cell phones, text messages, Internet service, BlackBerry technology, or fax machines. The only method of keeping up with the daughters and grandchildren was to send a messenger across miles of mountains over dusty trails, or to make the journey of several days, unannounced! Laban, however, knew that the eyes of the Lord were continually open and that He could continually see Jacob and the family. Laban said the Lord would "watch" over them. There are several different Hebrew words for the word *watch* in the English translation of the Old Testament. Some simply mean "to watch, to watch over, and to guard." This Hebrew word *watch* is *tsaphah*, which conveys the meaning of leaning forward and peering into the distance. When a person leans forward to see into the distance, that person is interested in what is occurring. The Mizpah covenant asks God to lean forward and look into the distance between Laban and Jacob and keep the family from danger.

What Is Mizpah?

According to the *Encyclopedia Judaica*, the word *Mizpah* (also spelled *Mizpeh*) is a "lookout point," or, as we would say in modern vernacular, *a watchtower*. The name Mizpah first appears in the Jacob story. The area later became a city that belonged to the tribe of Benjamin (Josh. 18:26). Throughout the early history of Israel, the name Mizpah appears at times in Scripture, and many events occurred in this area:

- The Israelites gathered at Mizpah to punish the men of Benjamin for their sins (Judg. 20–21).
- The prophet Samuel organized Israel to fight against the Philistines at Mizpah (1 Sam. 7:5).
- The area was fortified under the leadership of King Asa (1 Kings 15:22).
- Mizpah was the capital of the tribe of Judah when Jerusalem fell (2 Kings 25:23).

According to *Encyclopedia Judaica*, the traditional site of Mizpah was excavated from 1926 to 1932 by W. F. Bade and is located about eight miles north of Jerusalem. The close location of Mizpah to Jerusalem is important for several reasons. After twenty years in Syria, Jacob was returning to the Promised Land. The Syrian border would have been north of Canaan, near what is Lebanon today, and to the east, bordering Edom and Moab, which is the country of Jordan today. When Laban caught up with Jacob, he was about eight miles from what would one day be Jerusalem. This is interesting when considering that a person must go *out of their way* to travel from Syria to Jerusalem. The city is twenty-five hundred feet in elevation and surrounded by high rugged mountains. It is quite possible that Jacob intended on taking his caravan of wives, children, and servants to the area of Mount Moriah when his journey was interrupted by Laban. The reason may have been Jacob's *family link* to the area known as Mount Moriah, which was also the mountain where the future Jewish temple would be built by Solomon.

It was in Jerusalem that Jacob's grandfather Abraham met the first king and priest of the Most High God, Melchizedek, and gave the tithe to this righteous man (Gen. 14:20). Thus, the area (Jerusalem) was marked early in Hebrew history as a blessing for the Hebrew people. Second, it was in this area on Mount Moriah where Jacob's father, Isaac, was laid upon an altar and offered to God by his father, Abraham (Gen. 22:1–11). The third, and perhaps the most important, reason is the fact that it is believed by Jewish tradition that twenty years earlier, when Jacob was on the run from his brother, Esau, Jacob headed to Jerusalem (Mount Moriah) and experienced the famous dream of the angels ascending and descending from heaven on the ladder that stretched from the ground into heaven itself.

Now Jacob went out from Beersheba and went toward
Haran. So he came to a certain place and stayed there
all night, because the sun had set. And he took one of
the stones of that place and put it at his head, and he
lay down in that place to sleep. Then he dreamed, and
behold, a ladder was set up on the earth, and its top
reached to heaven; and there the angels of God were
ascending and descending on it.

—Genesis 28:10–12

During this dream, God told Jacob:

I am the Lord God of Abraham your father and the
God of Isaac; the land on which you lie I will give to
you and your descendants. Also your descendants shall
be as the dust of the earth; you shall spread abroad to
the west and the east, to the north and the south; and
in you and in your seed all the families of the earth
shall be blessed. Behold, I am with you and will keep
you wherever you go, and will bring you back to this
land; for I will not leave you until I have done what I
have spoken to you.

—Genesis 28:13–15

The Bible mentions a book called the "Book of Jasher"
(Josh. 10:13; 2 Sam. 1:18). A Hebrew scroll was discovered
and translated in the 1800s, which is called by some transla-
tors the "Book of Jasher." It is not considered inspired like the
Scriptures, but it is considered sacred Jewish history. We read
about the events occurring when Jacob is fleeing from Esau:

And Jacob went forth continuing his road to Haran, and
he came as far as mount Moriah, and he tarried there

all night near the city of Luz; and the Lord appeared there unto Jacob on that night, and he said unto him, I am the Lord God of Abraham and the God of Isaac thy father; the land upon which thou liest I will give unto thee and thy seed.

—JASHER 30:1[1]

Even without this passage, which states that the dream occurred at Mount Moriah, the biblical text indicates that the place where Jacob experienced the dream of the heavenly ladder was near Mount Moriah in Jerusalem. When Jacob awoke from the dream, he said, "This is none other than the house of God, and this is the gate of heaven" (Gen. 28:17). The phrase "house of God" in Hebrew is *bethel*. In Israel, the traditional site of Bethel is located near Jerusalem, but the Hebrew word *bethel* is also a general word meaning "house of God." The main clue to the location where Jacob and Laban met and established the Mizpah covenant is when Jacob said, "This is the gate of heaven" (Gen. 28:17). Biblically and in Jewish thought, the "gate of heaven" is the Temple Mount in Jerusalem, where hundreds of years after Jacob's death, Solomon constructed the first sacred temple of God in Jerusalem. Mount Moriah is recognized as the gate

> ALLOW THE MIZPAH COVENANT TO ESTABLISH THE *GATE OF HEAVEN* IN YOUR FAMILY'S LIFE, WHICH WILL ENABLE GOD'S ANGELS TO ASCEND AND DESCEND FROM HEAVEN AS THEY PROVIDE GOD'S PROTECTION TO YOUR FAMILY.

of heaven because, in the ancient temple, the burnt offerings ascended to the heavenly temple and were a sweet fragrance to the Lord. The temple incense was offered each morning on the golden altar as the prayers of the people ascended to heaven from the smoke of the incense. The temple of Solomon was built on Mount Moriah (2 Chron. 3:1), called the "Mount of the LORD" (Gen. 22:14). Thus, this area was the gate, or entrance, into heaven.

I SHALL RETURN

Before Jacob went to Syria, God visited him in the dream of the ladder and gave him the same promise given to his grandfather Abraham and his father, Isaac. God promised that all of the land of Canaan belonged to him and his children after him. In order to fulfill this promise of a nation being born in the Promised Land, this unmarried man, Jacob, knew he must return in the future and settle in the land he was leaving. Thus, he made a promise (vow) to God, saying:

> Then Jacob made a vow, saying, "If God will be with me, and keep me in this way that I am going, and give me bread to eat and clothing to put on, so that I come back to my father's house in peace, then the LORD shall be my God. And this stone which I have set as a pillar shall be God's house, and of all that You give me I will surely give a tenth to You."
>
> —GENESIS 28:20–22

Here we see a stone pillar marking the location where Jacob saw the bottom of the ladder and where he predicted this pillar one day would be God's house. The only house of God that the Hebrew people ever knew in their entire history that was constructed in or around Jerusalem was the two temples that once sat on Mount Moriah. Jacob also promised God "a tenth," which in Hebrew is the tithe on his blessings. This promise is also a prophetic indication that this future house of God would be the place where the tithe from Jacob's descendants would be presented to God.

The location of Mizpah, according to archeologists, was only eight miles from Jerusalem. It is now easy to understand why Jacob was apparently heading to Mount Moriah when his father-in-law, Laban, caught up with him. Jacob remembered his twenty-year-old vow to God, and I believe he was taking the family to the very place where he and God made the covenant of blessing. On his way, he was interrupted by a surprise visit from Laban!

THE ANGELS SHOW UP

After Jacob made the Mizpah covenant with Laban and made sacrifices, he and his brethren remained on the mountain all night. The following morning, Laban kissed his daughters and the grandchildren and headed back to Syria (Gen. 31:54–55). After Laban departed, the covenant immediately went into operation. Jacob continued his journey and suddenly encountered a large host of angels of God:

> So Jacob went on his way, and the angels of God met him. When Jacob saw them, he said, "This is God's camp." And he called the name of that place Mahanaim.
> —GENESIS 32:1–2

The King James Version says, "This is God's host." The Hebrew word *host* here is *machaneh*, and it alludes to an encampment of travelers, soldiers, or troops. The Hebrew name *Mahanaim* is a word that means "double camp." This could allude to Jacob's understanding that he was in charge of one large camp of individuals, and the angels of the Lord formed a second camp that met him as he came near the location of the gate of heaven.

Jacob would soon meet Esau and was uncertain of the reception he would receive. He was very fearful and knew Esau could kill him and his entire family if he chose to do so. When Jacob saw Esau coming, he positioned his servants in front, Leah and her children next, and Rachel with Joseph in the back. I believe he thought that in case Esau killed his servants and Leah, along with part of the family, his favorite wife, Rachel, could escape!

As part of his restoration with Esau, Jacob had prepared a large present for his estranged brother:

> He selected a gift for his brother Esau: two hundred female goats and twenty male goats, two hundred ewes and twenty rams, thirty female camels with their young, forty cows and ten bulls, and twenty female donkeys and ten male donkeys.
>
> —GENESIS 32:13–15, NIV

The gift was a portion of the animals that Jacob had herded from Laban's farm. He had not stolen these animals. They were a part of his wages paid to him for working for twenty years.

Why did Jacob present this gift to Esau? When Jacob finally met face-to-face with Esau, he said this to him:

> And Jacob said, Nay, I pray thee, if now I have found
> grace in thy sight, then receive my present at my hand:
> for therefore I have seen thy face, as though I had seen
> the face of God, and thou wast pleased with me.
> —GENESIS 33:10, KJV

Jacob asked Esau to receive the "present" from him of these numerous animals. The Hebrew word here for *present* is *minchah*, the word later used occasionally in the Old Testament for a voluntary offering. This word is used early in the Torah when Moses wrote about Cain's offering of the fruits of the ground that were presented to God (Gen. 4:3–5). The best explanation for why Jacob gave the gift is that it was his desire to fulfill the vow he made to God twenty years earlier when he promised God that if He would bring him back to his father's house, "I will surely give a tenth to You" (Gen. 28:22).

At this time in Hebrew history, Melchizedek, the king-priest, was dead, and there was no temple or tabernacle in the entire nation. Yet it appears that Jacob was determined to give away a portion, possibly a tenth, as his offering to God, and he gave this present to his brother, Esau!

Hundreds of years after this event in the time of the tabernacle and temple, there were offerings presented to the priesthood that were not animal offerings but were considered bloodless and voluntary offerings, such as grain and oil offerings. These were also called *minchah* in Hebrew. (See Leviticus 2.)

WRESTLING FOR A BLESSING

After preparing this offering to present to Esau, and before Jacob met Esau, Jacob sent his family on ahead and spent the night alone. Suddenly he encountered one angel whose words and actions would forever change his life and destiny. We read:

> Then Jacob was left alone; and a Man wrestled with him until the breaking of day. Now when He saw that He did not prevail against him, He touched the socket of his hip; and the socket of Jacob's hip was out of joint as He wrestled with him. And He said, "Let Me go, for the day breaks." But he said, "I will not let You go unless You bless me!" So He said to him, "What is your name?" And he said, "Jacob." And He said, "Your name shall no longer be called Jacob, but Israel; for you have struggled with God and with men, and have prevailed."
>
> —GENESIS 32:24–28

This wonderful encounter occurred the night before Jacob came face-to-face with Esau. This angel of the Lord changed Jacob's name to *Israel* and touched his thigh, giving him a limp for the rest of his life. Jacob had always been on the run, and now his *limp hip* would slow him down so he could no longer run from men or from God!

When studying the life of Jacob, it is interesting to read the number of times and places where an angel or a host of angels were a part of his dreams and life:

- Jacob dreamed the dream of the ladder of blessing with the angels of God (Gen. 28:12).
- An angel visited him in Syria, telling him to return to the Promised Land (Gen. 31:11–13).
- The angels met him prior to meeting Esau (Gen. 32:1–2).

■ Jacob wrestled an angel of the Lord, thus
receiving a spiritual transformation (Gen.
32:24–25).

Just who were these angelic messengers, and why were they
continually involved in Jacob's life and destiny? To understand
the full meaning of these questions, we must move forward
from the Mizpah covenant to the time when Jacob was an old
man nearing death, having lived his final years with his sons
and their children in Egypt. Jacob was interested in adopting
Ephraim and Manasseh, Joseph's two sons who were born
in Egypt. A prayer that Jacob prayed over the two sons will
reveal the importance of angels in the life of Jacob and his
descendants.

Chapter 5

THE GUARDIAN OF THE PEOPLE OF GOD

The Angel who has redeemed me from all evil,
Bless the lads;
Let my name be named upon them,
And the name of my fathers Abraham and Isaac;
And let them grow into a multitude in the midst
   of the earth.

—GENESIS 48:16

T HIS SCENE UNFOLDS IN EGYPT. JACOB AND HIS SONS were living in the land of Goshen after being preserved during a seven-year global famine. The old patriarch knew he would die soon and his spirit would be gathered to his people (Gen. 49:33). In the tradition of his father, Isaac, and his grandfather Abraham, Jacob, now called Israel, requested the two sons of Joseph, both born in Egypt, to come to his bedside so he could pronounce the important and anticipated patriarchal blessing over the youths. As Jacob laid his hands upon the lads, he spoke the words above from Genesis 48:16.

At that moment, these two grandsons of Jacob were

officially adopted into the tribal listing of Israel. When the Hebrews later returned to the Promised Land, the tribes of Ephraim and Manasseh were both presented an inheritance in the form of land. Jacob's prayer was answered, and both tribes grew into a multitude and carried the name Israel with them.

In the prayer, Jacob asked God to permit the angel who redeemed him to bless the sons. What angel is Jacob speaking about that "redeemed [him] from all evil," and when was he "redeemed"? The Hebrew word for *redeemed* is *ga'al*, and it is the word used for the next of kin (called a *kinsman-redeemer*) who would redeem family property back that had been foreclosed upon or sold due to economic duress. For example, in the Book of Ruth, the Hebrew Naomi and her Gentile daughter-in-law Ruth were both widows and had lived in Moab. After ten years, both returned to Naomi's home in Bethlehem. Naomi had been away so long that she had lost her husband's land, and she had no power to get it back. She knew of one legal option: she requested that her dead husband's brother, Boaz, being a near kin, legally redeem back the rights to the property. Boaz would be a *ga'al*, a redeemer.

We have already reviewed the visitation of angels in Jacob's life. When Jacob was working for Laban in Syria, an angel appeared to him with the following revelation:

> Then the Angel of God spoke to me in a dream, saying, "Jacob." And I said, "Here I am." And He said, "Lift your eyes now and see, all the rams which leap on the flocks are streaked, speckled, and gray-spotted; for I have seen all that Laban is doing to you. I am the God of Bethel, where you anointed the pillar and where you

made a vow to Me. Now arise, get out of this land, and
return to the land of your family."

—GENESIS 31:11–13

This angel also protected Jacob from Laban by appearing
in the dream warning Laban not to speak evil or good of
Jacob, and the angel continued to observe and follow Jacob
throughout his life. The Lord had revealed to Jacob, "Behold,
I am with you and will keep you wherever you go, and will
bring you back to this land; for I will not leave you until I
have done what I have spoken to you" (Gen. 28:15).

God was promising to "keep" Jacob. The Hebrew word for
keep is *shamar,* the same word used in the confession called
the blessing of the priest, when he held up both hands over the
people and proclaimed, "The LORD bless you and keep you"
(Num. 6:24). The word means "to hedge about or to guard."
God was promising to protect Jacob wherever his journey took
him and to bring him back again to the land promised to
Abraham and Isaac.

THE ANGEL FOLLOWING ISRAEL

Eventually Jacob died, along with his twelve sons. However,
after four hundred years in Egypt (Gen. 15:13), the seventy
souls that came out of Jacob (Exod. 1:5) had become a multitude of six hundred thousand men of war (Exod. 12:37). As
Moses brought the nation of Israel out of Egypt, across the
Red Sea, and into the wilderness, he needed supernatural
assistance to complete this difficult assignment.

God gave a promise that a special angel would precede
Israel in the wilderness journey and assist him and the people

all the way to the Promised Land. This is the promise God revealed to Moses:

> Behold, I send an Angel before you to keep you in the way and to bring you into the place which I have prepared. Beware of Him and obey His voice; do not provoke Him, for He will not pardon your transgressions; for My name is in Him. But if you indeed obey His voice and do all that I speak, then I will be an enemy to your enemies and an adversary to your adversaries. For My Angel will go before you and bring you in to the Amorites and the Hittites and the Perizzites and the Canaanites and the Hivites and the Jebusites; and I will cut them off.
>
> —EXODUS 23:20–23

The angel that God identifies as "My Angel" was personally given the assignment to prepare the way, keep the people, and bring them into the Promised Land. This angel was never visibly seen by the Israelites during their forty-year journey, because he was concealed in a large pillar of cloud that settled over the camp of Israel by day and in a heavenly pillar of fire that hovered over the camp by night (Exod. 13:22). This angel, known as the angel of God's presence, dwelt with the Hebrew nation during the

> GOD HAS COMMISSIONED THE *ANGEL OF THE LORD* TO LEAD HIS HEAVENLY MESSENGERS AS THEY WORK TO DEFEND, KEEP, AND PROTECT HIS PEOPLE.

entire forty years. It was after the death of Moses that this invisible angel made a special appearance to Joshua.

THE "CAPTAIN OF THE LORD'S HOST"

After forty years, following the death of an unbelieving generation of Israelites, the children of those who died in the wilderness prepared to seize their inheritance from the numerous tribes dwelling on their promised soil. On an appointed day, the manna (bread from heaven), the cloud, and the fire at night ceased. Rising early in the morning, Joshua was preparing the fighting men of Israel to invade Jericho when he encountered a strange and unexpected visitor. Joshua observed a man standing near him, and he demanded to know if the stranger was for or against Israel. The man replied, "As captain of the host of the LORD am I now come" (Josh. 5:14, KJV). This man was in reality a heavenly messenger sent to assist Joshua in the conquest of their first city, Jericho. The angelic visitor made an unusual demand to Joshua:

> Then the Commander of the LORD's army said to Joshua, "Take your sandal off your foot, for the place where you stand is holy." And Joshua did so.
>
> —JOSHUA 5:15

This statement is similar to the command the Almighty gave to Moses more than forty-one years earlier, prior to Moses returning to Egypt to deliver Israel from Egyptian slavery. God said to Moses, "Take your sandals off your feet, for the place where you stand is holy ground" (Exod. 3:5). The King James Version clearly indicates that God instructed Moses to remove his "shoes" and Joshua his "shoe." Some would suggest there is no significance between shoes (plural) and shoe (singular). I would kindly disagree.

In Moses's case, the Lord Himself appeared, and in Joshua's case, the captain of the Lord's army appeared. In both cases the men of God are informed that they are on "holy ground." There is a difference between removing shoes and taking off a single shoe. In ancient Hebrew history, when a man died and the wife had lost the property (because of debt, taxes, and so forth), she could legally redeem her inheritance back through a near relative of her husband, called a *kinsman-redeemer.* Part of the process was for the nearest kin to present his shoe to the elders of the city at the city gates. After a special procedure, he exchanged his shoe, which gave permission for the near kin to take back the lost property. This occurred when Boaz presented his shoe in Bethlehem on behalf of his dead brother's wife, Naomi:

> Now this was the custom in former times in Israel concerning redeeming and exchanging, to confirm anything: one man took off his sandal and gave it to the other, and this was a confirmation in Israel. Therefore the close relative said to Boaz, "Buy it for yourself." So he took off his sandal.
>
> —Ruth 4:7–8

This captain of the Lord's army was asking Joshua to present him his shoe, thus giving the angel permission to go before the children of Israel and prepare the way for God's chosen people to retake the land that had been controlled by the Canaanites for about four hundred forty years while Israel was dwelling in Egypt. I believe this angel of the Lord was the very angel that appeared to Abraham when he was about to sacrifice Isaac (Gen. 22:11), when Eleazar was searching for a bride for Isaac (Gen. 24:7), and again when Jacob returned to the Promised Land (Gen. 31:11–13).

The Lord certainly watched over Jacob, his wives, and his twelve sons. The same angels of the Lord that followed the ancient patriarchs of the faith are presently a part of the heavenly host and are still active in protecting the people of the Most High God.

According to Scripture, the main protecting angel for Israel is named Michael. We read where he contended with Satan over the body of Moses shortly after Moses's death (Jude 9). The prophet Daniel identified Michael as "the great prince who stands watch over the sons of your people [Israel]" (Dan. 12:1). In the future Great Tribulation, Michael and a host of his angels will engage in a cosmic conflict, resulting in the expulsion of Satan and his evil angels out of the second heaven down to the earth (Rev. 12:7–10). Michael has been given a high ranking among the angels, being called an "archangel" (Jude 9). He is given special authority in dealing with evil powers and guarding Israel.

Usually, when Michael is involved in any biblical activity, he is mentioned by name. The angel of God's presence that ministered to Abraham and continued to follow the Hebrew nation until they repossessed the Promised Land is never named. A few may suggest that this angel was actually Michael, and others believe he was the preincarnate Christ.

HIS NAME IS "SECRET"

One reason why some theologians suggest that the angel of the Lord in the Old Testament was Christ is because of an interesting statement in Judges 13. The Israelites were in a cycle of bondage and captivity to their internal and external enemies. God would raise up deliverers called *judges* to direct wars and deliver Israel from the hands of her adversaries. One such deliverer was Samson.

Prior to Samson's birth, an angel of the Lord appeared to Samson's mother and informed her that she would conceive a son who would be a Nazirite. A Nazirite vow is recorded in Numbers 6:2–8. The son to be born a Nazirite could never drink strong drink, never touch a dead carcass, and never cut his hair. Samson's father, Manoah, was thrilled at the announcement of the birth of a son and desired to make a large meal. He invited the visitor who had announced his son's birth to dinner. (He did not realize it was an angel because he came in the form of a man—Judges 13:15–16.)

It was then that Manoah asked the angel for his name:

> And Manoah said unto the angel of the LORD, What is thy name, that when thy sayings come to pass we may do thee honour? And the angel of the LORD said unto him, Why askest thou thus after my name, seeing it is secret?
> —JUDGES 13:17–18, KJV

When reading this passage, the angel said his name was "secret." In English, this would mean it cannot be told because it is a secret and should remain a mystery. The word *secret* is found fifty-two times in the Old Testament and basically means "something hidden." This word *secret* in Judges 13:18, however, is a different Hebrew word, *pil'iy*, and can be translated "wonderful." In Isaiah 9:6 there is a prophecy concerning the Messiah in which Isaiah predicted, "His name will be called Wonderful," which is from a Hebrew word meaning miracle. This angel was saying his name was Wonderful, which is similar to the name given to the Messiah! Because of such unique links, some suggest that the angel may have actually been a manifestation of Christ prior to His incarnation.

A second example is found in Daniel 10, when Daniel saw what scholars call a *theophany*. The word in Greek is *theophaneia*, meaning an appearance or a showing of God. It alludes to the many appearances of God in the Old Testament and emphasizes the fact that men were able to see God when He would appear in some form (Exod. 3:3–6; 19:16–25). We read in Daniel 10:

> Now on the twenty-fourth day of the first month, as I was by the side of the great river, that is, the Tigris, I lifted my eyes and looked, and behold, a certain man clothed in linen, whose waist was girded with gold of Uphaz! His body was like beryl, his face like the appearance of lightning, his eyes like torches of fire, his arms and feet like burnished bronze in color, and the sound of his words like the voice of a multitude.
>
> —Daniel 10:4–6

Now, compare this manifestation of a divine being with John's vision of Christ in the heavenly temple:

> Then I turned to see the voice that spoke with me. And having turned I saw seven golden lampstands, and in the midst of the seven lampstands One like the Son

of Man, clothed with a garment down to the feet and girded about the chest with a golden band. His head and hair were white like wool, as white as snow, and His eyes like a flame of fire; His feet were like fine brass, as if refined in a furnace, and His voice as the sound of many waters; He had in His right hand seven stars, out of His mouth went a sharp two-edged sword, and His countenance was like the sun shining in its strength. And when I saw Him, I fell at His feet as dead.

—REVELATION 1:12–17

Consider these comparisons:

- Both are clothed in linen.
- Both have a golden girdle.
- The countenance of both was like lightning or the sun.
- They had brass feet.
- The voice of each was like a multitude or many waters.

Whether the angel of the Lord was a ministering spirit, a theophany, or Michael the archangel, we may never know. We can, however, be assured that God commissioned His heavenly messengers to defend, keep, and protect His people, Israel.

Chapter 6

ANGELS—HEAVENLY ASSIGNMENTS FOR EARTHLY PEOPLE

> The angel of the LORD encamps all around
>   those who fear Him,
> And delivers them.
>
> —PSALM 34:7

> For He shall give His angels charge over you,
> To keep you in all your ways.
> In their hands they shall bear you up,
> Lest you dash your foot against a stone.
> You shall tread upon the lion and the cobra,
> The young lion and the serpent you shall
>   trample underfoot.
>
> —PSALM 91:11–13

ANGELS—EITHER YOU BELIEVE THEY EXIST, OR YOU consider them the belief of religious people who either are deceived or have a wild imagination. If you believe in the Scriptures, it is impossible to deny the numerous references to these heavenly messengers and their numerous assignments.

They are not only mentioned in the Old Testament, but they were also very involved in Christ's earthly ministry:

- Angels announced the birth of Christ (Luke 1:26–38).
- An angel told Joseph to take Mary as his wife (Matt. 1:20).
- An angel warned wise men not to return to Herod (Matt. 2:12).
- An angel warned Joseph to flee to Egypt (Matt. 2:13).
- Angels ministered to Christ after His temptation (Matt. 4:11).
- An angel brought healing at the pool of Bethesda (John 5:4).
- Angels ministered to Christ in Gethsemane (Luke 22:43).
- Angels were present at the Resurrection (Luke 24:4).
- Angels announced that Christ would return again (Acts 1:10–11).

When Christ taught His disciples how to pray, He introduced a prayer called the Lord's Prayer. One line in this beautiful prayer has always stood out to me. It is the phrase, "Thy will be done in earth, as it is in heaven" (Matt. 6:10, KJV). Jesus was praying for *God's kingdom* to come and for God's will to be done on the earth. Christ spoke often of the kingdom and gave a series of parables that scholars call *the parables of the kingdom.* (See Matthew 13.) He also gave a revealing statement concerning those who would enter the kingdom:

> From the days of John the Baptist until now, the
> kingdom of heaven has been forcefully advancing, and
> forceful men lay hold of it.
>
> —MATTHEW 11:12, NIV

In Christ's time there were numerous customs and traditions established among the Jewish religious leaders, specifically the Pharisees. The "tradition of the elders" (Mark 7:3) included cooking meals and washing all pots and pans before the sun set on the Sabbath day. The disciples were once rebuked for eating without washing their hands, since the belief among the Pharisees was that if people ate with unwashed hands, they could swallow demonic spirits. These religious zealots believed it was a sin to heal the sick on the Sabbath day, and they rebuked Christ for breaking the Sabbath by telling a man to "take up [his] bed and walk" (John 5:8). Thus, the common people in Christ's day made extreme efforts at times to seek the touch of Christ, knowing the religious leaders would attack them for doing so. Thus they "forced their way" into the kingdom by breaking the traditions of the elders. A woman with the issue of blood and an unclean leper broke through and touched Christ. Both were forbidden to be in public with their physical infirmities, yet they made a decision to seek out Christ for healing. Healing was a promise in both covenants, and the traditions of men had hindered multitudes from receiving the benefits promised by God (Ps. 103). It became necessary for those in need to make a risky decision. Do they remain in their bondage just to keep the status quo happy? Or do they stir up opposition and reach out and take hold of the promise? Those who received their miracles forced their way past man's opinions. Through Christ, God's will in heaven was being done on Earth.

In order for God to perform His will on Earth, He often uses His heavenly messengers—angels—to reveal His will to certain people or to initiate judgments upon the ungodly so that His will won't be hindered. Two examples of angels performing acts of judgment on Earth are found in both Testaments.

In 2 Kings 19, the Assyrian king Sennacherib marched his army toward Judea to seize the territory and take the Jews as captive. King Hezekiah took all the gold and silver from the temple in Jerusalem and gave it to Sennacherib, including the gold covering on the temple doors (2 Kings 18:13–16). The Assyrians were so bold that they spoke in Hebrew and told the Jews that God had sent them to destroy Judea and Jerusalem. Then they mocked the Hebrew God and said, "Has there ever been a god anywhere who delivered anyone from the king of Assyria?...So what makes you think that GOD can save Jerusalem from me?" (2 Kings 18:33–35, THE MESSAGE). This blasphemous threat concerned the Judean king, Hezekiah, who contacted the prophet Isaiah to conduct an urgent prayer meeting and beseech God to intervene to spare Judea

> IN ORDER TO PERFORM HIS WILL ON EARTH, GOD OFTEN USES HIS HEAVENLY MESSENGERS TO REVEAL HIS WILL TO HIS PEOPLE AND TO INITIATE JUDGMENTS UPON THOSE WHO WOULD ATTEMPT TO HINDER HIS WILL.

and Jerusalem. The prayer reached the heavenly temple, and God dispatched one of His angels to march at night through the camp of the Assyrians. Here are the results:

> And it came to pass on a certain night that the angel of the LORD went out, and killed in the camp of the Assyrians one hundred and eighty-five thousand; and when people arose early in the morning, there were the corpses—all dead. So Sennacherib king of Assyria departed and went away, returned home, and remained at Nineveh.
>
> —2 KINGS 19:35–36

The Jewish historian Flavius Josephus writes about what occurred that night in Jerusalem:

> Now when Sennacherib was returning from his Egyptian war to Jerusalem, he found his army under Rabshakeh his general in danger [by a plague], for God had sent a pestilential distemper upon his army; and on the very first night of the siege, a hundred fourscore and five thousand, with their captains and generals, were destroyed. So the king was in a great dread and in a terrible agony at this calamity; and being in great fear for his whole army, he fled with the rest of his forces.
>
> —*ANTIQUITIES OF THE JEWS*,
> BOOK 10, CHAPTER 1, SECTION 5

In this historical narrative, one angel from the Lord slew 185,000 men in one night. Christ informed His disciples that He could commission twelve legions of angels to assist and deliver Him prior to His death (Matt. 26:53). In Christ's time, the Roman armies were divided into units. For example:

- ▪ Eight men made one unit.
- ▪ Ten units (80 men) made one century.
- ▪ Six centuries (480 men) made one cohort.
- ▪ Ten cohorts (4,800 men) made one legion.
- ▪ It took 5,280 soldiers to make one army.

If Christ could have called upon twelve legions of angels, and a common legion was 4,800 men, then twelve legions of angels would be 57,600 individual angels! If one angel could destroy an army of 185,000 men, then 57,600 angels, each taking out 185,000 men, could destroy a total of 10,656,000,000 men! That is more people than now live on Earth. Is it any wonder that when the Syrian army surrounded the mountain to capture Elisha, and the horses of fire and chariots of fire surrounded the prophet, the man of God told his servant, "There are more for us than there are against us." (See 2 Kings 6:14–17.) As an additional note, if Satan drew one-third of the angelic host to follow him (Rev. 12:4), then there are two angels on our side for every one opposing angel that would be against us!

ANGELS SENDING JUDGMENT

The New Testament records an unusual event involving an angel who brought judgment against a national leader. Luke records a political event where as Herod sat upon his throne, the people screamed that he was not a man but a god (Acts 12:20–22). The historian Josephus wrote about the event also with these words:

> On the second day of which shows he put on a garment made wholly of silver, and of a contexture

truly wonderful, and came into the theater early in the morning; at which time the silver of his garment being illuminated by the fresh reflection of the sun's rays upon it, shone out after a surprising manner, and was so resplendent as to spread a horror over those that looked intently upon him; and presently his flatterers cried out...that he was a god...the king did neither rebuke them....A severe pain also arose in his belly, and began in a most violent manner.

—*ANTIQUITIES OF THE JEWS*,
Book 19, Chapter 8, Section 2

Luke recorded that when the people glorified Herod as a god, an "angel of the Lord struck him, because he did not give glory to God. And he was eaten by worms" (Acts 12:23). Josephus reported that the pains became violent, and in five days the king was dead at age fifty-four. We don't often picture angels as being initiators of God's judgment, but in the Book of Revelation, John reports seeing angels pouring out the judgments during the Great Tribulation (Rev. 8:2; 15:1). God's will in heaven is performed on Earth and is often linked to the assignments given to angels. While angels may bring judgment upon the ungodly and wicked, they will also bring warnings to the righteous.

WARNINGS IN DREAMS OR VISIONS

Throughout the Scriptures, angelic messengers often appear in dreams or visions, revealing warnings or the plans and purposes of God. Often when a prophetic message was to be released from God's throne to men on Earth, it was sent through an angel of the Lord. In Jewish and early church tradition, it is believed there are seven chief angels:

1. Michael—the archangel over Israel
2. Gabriel—the angel over Gentile powers
3. Raphael—the angel in charge of the prayers of the saints
4. Uriel—the angel in charge of the underworld
5. Jeremiel—duties are not mentioned
6. Raquel—the angel who brings judgment
7. Sariel—duties are not mentioned

In Scripture, two angels are specifically named. One is the archangel Michael (Jude 9), a strong fighting prince who has numerous angels under his command (Rev. 12:7). The second named angel is Gabriel. In Scripture, Gabriel is the angel of God's presence (Luke 1:19) and is always linked to bringing forth divine revelations, such as the interpretation of prophetic visions or dreams. Gabriel was the angel who was commanded to make Daniel understand the strange visions of the future he was receiving (Dan. 8:16; 9:21) and was the heavenly messenger announcing the conception of John the Baptist and Christ (Luke 1:19, 26). Michael is an angel linked to Israel, and Gabriel is often linked to the Gentile nations.

On other occasions, angels would visit through visions and dreams. However, the actual names of the heavenly visitors are not listed in the Scriptures:

▪ An angel from heaven spoke to Abraham, telling him not to slay Isaac on the altar (Gen. 22:11).

- An angel blocked the path of Balaam when he was preparing to curse Israel (Num. 22:22).
- An angel appeared to Gideon to direct him in battle (Judg. 6:12).
- An angel appeared to Samson's mother, predicting the birth of a son (Judg. 13:3).
- An angel stretched his hand over Jerusalem to destroy it (2 Sam. 24:16).
- An angel strengthened the prophet Elijah (1 Kings 19:5).
- An angel shut the mouth of the lions, thus protecting Daniel (Dan. 6:22).
- An angel revealed numerous prophetic revelations to Zechariah (Zech. 1–6).

My father, an ordained minister of the gospel for nearly sixty years, has experienced numerous dreams (and occasional visions) throughout his lifetime that were warnings of danger and revealed either the plans and strategies of the adversary or the harmful intentions of wicked and carnal individuals, some secretly hindering the work of God. At times in warning dreams, he was addressed by a man who called him "son." In fact, at numerous times he related the experience of a dream or a strange *night vision* and told me how a man in the dream had called him "son." He always told me that in a spiritual dream, if the messenger was either the Lord or an angel of the Lord, he often addressed a man by saying "son" and a woman by saying "daughter." These words, *son* and *daughter*, identify the intimate family relationship between God our Father and His children—His sons and daughters.

PROTECTED IN VIETNAM

During the Vietnam War in the 1960s, my dad's brother Lewis was sent to the front line of battle. Lewis was with the Lima Company of marines. My father was pastor of a small rural congregation in Big Stone Gap, Virginia. Lewis was always on Dad's heart and mind, and Dad continually asked God for protection for his brother.

One night, Dad lay in bed silently praying for Lewis. Suddenly, Dad saw a bright light come through the window shade. He thought perhaps it was a car passing by and continued to pray. Within a few minutes, Dad suddenly experienced a full-color vision that appeared to be taking place somewhere in Vietnam. In the vision, he saw a group of marines who were digging a trench. In front of them were some high grass and several trees. Dad saw three snakes with rifles strapped on them crawling toward the marines. He heard gunfire and saw a man fall to the ground. Suddenly, he came out of the vision and began praying for Lewis. He sat down and wrote a letter, giving Lewis the details of the vision, including a description of the area. Amazingly, the letter reached Lewis, who kept it in his military fatigues.

Shortly after reading Dad's letter, Lewis and a group of marines were digging a trench, and Lewis looked around, realizing the area was identical to the same place that Dad described in the vision. By instinct, he suddenly threw himself back into the trench as enemy gunfire broke the silence. The point man standing in front of Lewis was killed. In a letter sent to Dad, Lewis wrote about the incident and asked Dad,

"How do you do it?" wondering how he saw those things before they occurred.

ANOTHER UNCLE SPARED FROM DEATH

In the mid 1980s, Dad was in deep prayer and saw a vision of an accident. He clearly saw a coal truck hitting a vehicle head-on, and he saw that the person sitting on the passenger side had been decapitated. He sensed it was a warning for his brother Morgan, who lived in West Virginia. Dad went to the phone and attempted to call Morgan several times but to no avail. He told Mom, "I am going to the church to pray, and don't let anyone bother me under any circumstance." Dad described to me that he interceded under such a heavy prayer burden that his stomach muscles began to hurt. He was pleading with God to spare his brother's life.

After one hour, he heard the Holy Spirit tell him, "Son, you are asking Me to spare the life of one who has known Me but willfully has chosen to turn from Me. He is not walking in covenant with Me." This caused Dad to pray even more intently for another thirty minutes, asking God to extend His mercy to Morgan. It was then that Dad heard the Holy Spirit speak to him again, saying, "When you pastored in Northern Virginia, I showed you an angel that would be with you when you needed him. If you will ask the Father to send your angel to protect your brother, He will do so." Dad began to ask the Lord to send a protective angel to wherever Morgan was at that time.

It was later that evening when Dad got Morgan on the phone and told him that he had prayed for him to be spared from death. Morgan related this story to Dad: That morning he and a friend had gone to town and were returning home in his truck. Morgan felt a strange urge to stop at a small restaurant and get a soda. Morgan's neighbors, who lived across the street, were following them in a car and passed them as Morgan's truck turned into the restaurant parking lot. A few minutes later, both men were on the road heading home. To their shock, as they rounded a curve a mile up the road, they discovered that a large coal truck had struck the car with the neighbors, killing them both and decapitating the woman passenger. Dad said, "Morgan, that was intended for you, but the Lord sent His angel to have you stop for a few minutes so you would not be on the path of that huge coal truck!" This incident brought Morgan into a restored relationship with the Lord.

Many reading this book may think that your escape from danger or death during war, times of drug abuse, or accidents may have been *luck*. However, if you will investigate, in most cases you will discover that someone, somewhere, was burdened for you and was praying for your safety and protection.

WARNING DREAMS OF COMING TROUBLE

Angels are also involved in bringing warnings of coming danger to God's people. After the wise men from the east brought their gifts to baby Jesus in Bethlehem, they were warned in a dream not to return to Jerusalem to report to Herod about the infant's birth. God knew that Herod was planning on executing the children under two years of age living in the area. Any report from the wise men would tip Herod off to the exact location of the infant king of the Jews (Matt. 2:7–12).

Immediately afterward, an angel of the Lord appeared to Joseph, the husband of Mary, and warned him not to remain in the area but to take the young infant, Jesus, and His mother and go to Egypt for a season (Matt. 2:13–14). The departure to Egypt prevented Herod from killing Jesus. I also believe the young couple may have used the gold, frankincense, and myrrh provided by the wise men to provide for their needs while living in Egypt (Matt. 2:11).

Many years ago, I experienced a warning dream related to some form of spiritual attack I would encounter. In this dream, I was standing at a very large lake of beautiful clear water, fishing with a large fishing pole. Suddenly, I caught the largest fish I had ever caught. As I reeled it in and my hands were removing the fishhook, the large beautiful fish became a large serpent. I immediately threw the serpent to the ground, and it rose up and bit me on my forehead and on my feet. I suddenly picked up the serpent and threw it back into the lake, and as it began to go back into the water, it became a large fish again. I heard a voice speak in the dream and say, "The serpent will bite you, but it won't kill you." I knew that one day I would go back to this same lake and catch the fish again, but there would be some form of attack against my ministry and me in the days ahead.

Months later, I was ministering in a large church, and the meeting had continued for many weeks. It was the largest meeting with the best spiritual results I had ever experienced. At the conclusion of the meeting, there was an unexpected attack of the enemy that occurred that affected two things: my mind and my ministry. The serpent had bit me on my head and my feet. I was very upset, and the lies and rumors that some people spread caused men to cancel my meetings with them in some churches (this was the serpent's bite on my feet). My ministry was being disrupted by a sly verbal attack directed by the adversary. However, even though the enemy intended it for evil, God eventually turned it around, and I returned to this church and ministered on many occasions.

The meaning of the warning dream was this: The lake represented a large church, and the fish was the harvest of souls, for Christ said we would be "fishers of men" (Matt. 4:19). The revival resulted in hundreds of converts (the large fish), but the adversary attacked the meeting, and thus the serpent (representing a satanic attack) manifested. The snake-bite was on my head (my thoughts) and my feet (my traveling ministry, for the feet spread the gospel—Rom. 10:15). When the snake was thrown in the water and became a fish, this indicated that when the battle was concluded, I would return to the same lake (church) and get the harvest back.

It is important to note that not all dreams—in fact, few dreams—are spiritual dreams from the Lord but are just dreams. However, when a dream contains symbolism found in the Bible and it greatly troubles you for many days, it may indicate a warning or a message from the Lord.

THE SPEED OF ANGELS

Throughout Scripture, we can see that numerous duties and responsibilities were given to the angels of the Lord. There are many angels assigned to minister before the throne of God. We know there are cherubim that are guardians of the presence of God. Isaiah saw seraphim with six wings on each side, crying,

"Holy is the LORD" (Isa. 6:1–3). John, in Revelation, revealed there were "living creatures" with four faces—a calf, lion, eagle, and man—full of eyes, saying, "Holy, holy, holy" continually before the throne of the God (Rev. 4:7–8). The most common angels are simply *ministering spirits* that are sent to minister to those who are the heirs of salvation (Heb. 1:14).

I have always been fascinated with the difference between an earthly body and a spirit body. In an earthly body of flesh and blood, we are restricted. We can only travel at certain speeds, such as in the pressurized compartment of a military jet or spacecraft. If the speed (g-forces) were to be increased, the pressure would peel the flesh from our bodies. We are also unable to move through solids, such as a wall. The spirit world, however, is not limited to human restrictions. Angels are spirits and can move faster than the speed of light.

Ezekiel saw cherubim moving in the heavens and said they "ran back and forth, in appearance like a flash of lightning" (Ezek. 1:13–14). Light travels at 186,000 miles per second. The earth is approximately 25,000 miles in circumference at the equator. This means that light could travel around the earth nearly 7.5 times in just one second (186,000 miles per second divided by 25,000). In the earthly realm, if angels can travel at the speed of light, then they can arrive on the scene in your time of difficulty the moment you say, "Help!"

Let me add that a spirit is not restricted to walls, doors, or other objects. Even Christ in His resurrected body could walk through a door that was locked (John 20:19). There is one type of *transportation* faster than the speed of light, and it's the speed of thought. The spirit world can actually travel at the speed of thought, which is presently impossible to determine. Angelic beings can be at the throne in heaven and immediately be in the atmosphere above the earth. When the angel appeared to Daniel and informed him that for twenty-one days the answer to his prayer had been hindered by a demonic spirit in the air, the angel said, "Since the first day you began to pray...your request has been heard in heaven. I have come in answer to your prayer" (Dan. 10:12, NLT). Daniel's words ascended from Babylon and were heard the same day in heaven. The angel was coming on the same day to bring the answer but was restrained by the evil prince spirit over Persia (Dan. 10:13). Angels can travel from the highest part of the heaven at the edge of the universe to Earth and back by simply thinking about where they desire to go.

> GOD LOVES CHILDREN SO MUCH THAT HE ASSIGNS PROTECTIVE, GUARDIAN ANGELS TO WATCH OVER THEM AND PROTECT THEM FROM HARM.

THE ASSIGNMENTS GIVEN TO ANGELS

There are several interesting facts about angels found throughout the Scriptures. These include:

- Angels need no rest (Rev. 4:8).
- Angels can be visible and invisible (Num. 22:22; Heb. 13:2).
- Angels can descend to Earth and ascend to heaven (Gen. 28:12; John 1:51).

- Angels have a language of their own (1 Cor. 13:1).
- Angels are innumerable (Heb. 12:22).
- Angels wear white garments (John 20:12).
- Angels eat food called *manna* (Ps. 78:25).
- Angels can appear in human form at times (Heb. 13:2).

Throughout the Bible we read of the duties that are given to the angels. I will list just a few of the many duties found in Scripture. These include:

- Guarding gates (Rev. 21:12)
- Guarding the tree of life (Gen. 3:24)
- Guarding the bottomless pit (Rev. 20:1–2)
- Bringing the righteous to paradise at death (Luke 16:22)
- Executing judgment on the unrighteous (Rev. 15:1–16)
- Assisting in giving the Law to Moses (Heb. 2:2)
- Separating the good from the bad at judgment (Matt. 13:39–41)
- Gathering the elect after the Tribulation (Matt. 24:31)

It is important to discover how angels are involved in the lives of believers from a more personal and practical level. The Lord is concerned about every area of our lives. Christ mentioned how the Father sees a raven feeding and watches the lilies grow in the field, and if He cares for the birds and the flowers, He certainly is concerned about us (Luke 12:24–28).

ANGELS ARE ASSIGNED TO CHILDREN

Take heed that you do not despise one of these little
ones, for I say to you that in heaven their angels always
see the face of My Father who is in heaven.

—MATTHEW 18:10

Children were attracted to Christ during His earthly ministry.
Parents brought their children to Christ and requested that He
lay His hands upon them and bless them (Mark 10:13). This
was an ancient custom among the patriarchs (Abraham, Isaac,
and Jacob). It was also common for parents to request that a
righteous man, such as a noted rabbi, offer a special prayer on
behalf of their children. The disciples were displeased with the
many parents who were bringing their children to Jesus, and
on one occasion, they attempted to prevent the moms and
dads from this blessing prayer (Mark 10:13–14).

Christ asked His followers who they thought was the
greatest in the kingdom (Matt. 18:1). He called a child to
Himself and said, "Assuredly, I say to you, unless you are
converted and become as little children, you will by no means
enter the kingdom of heaven. Therefore whoever humbles
himself as this little child is the greatest in the kingdom of
heaven" (Matt. 18:3–4). I tell congregations that Christ said
be childlike and not childish! Christ's love for the children is
also demonstrated in the warning He gave immediately after
this verse:

Whoever receives one little child like this in My name
receives Me. But whoever causes one of these little ones
who believe in Me to sin, it would be better for him if

> a millstone were hung around his neck, and he were
> drowned in the depth of the sea.
>
> —MATTHEW 18:5–6

Four verses later, Jesus revealed that the little children have angels that He calls "their angels." He revealed that these guardian angels are always beholding the face of the heavenly Father. It is a serious offense for a person, especially an adult, to harm a little one physically, emotionally, or spiritually. The phrase "little ones" is mentioned six times in the King James Version of the New Testament (Matt. 10:42; 18:6, 10, 14; Mark 9:42; Luke 17:2). The Greek word for "little" is *mikros*, and it alludes to something that is little or the least.

During my earlier ministry, I heard pastors make the statement that they did not want to spend money sending buses or vans to pick up children since many were poor and could not give to support the church. In my opinion, such a statement offends a little one. Some pastors just do not have a shepherd's heart.

We often hear of a man or a woman abusing his or her own children, either physically or mentally, causing bodily harm and permanent emotional damage to the child.

As a teenage evangelist in the late 1970s, I recall ministering in Virginia. Being a teenager, my young ministry attracted large numbers of young people my age and younger who would often attend the revivals just to hear someone their own age preach. On several occasions, a teenager from another denomination would answer the altar call and receive a definite spiritual experience, only to return home and be lambasted by one or both parents. I will never forget a day in May 1979 when one man, a deacon in a mainline church in Richmond, Virginia, told the pastor of a church where I was preaching, "I'd rather see my child go to hell than to be attending a revival at a church that was not the same denomination as mine." This is the same spirit that the *sons of thunder* (James and John) had when they requested Jesus to burn down the city of Samaria for preventing Jesus from ministering in the city (Luke 9:51–54).

When my father pastored in Northern Virginia, one of his church members, who was ex-military, occasionally traveled to local churches to preach in special meetings. He told Dad of one occasion when two beautiful children who had been invited to a church service answered the altar call and were on their knees asking Christ into their hearts at the front of the church. Their unbelieving father, who had been informed that the children were in the sanctuary, drove to the church, stormed down the aisle, jerked his children up from the altar, and told them they were coming home with him immediately. When the minister attempted to calm the dad down and told him the seriousness of his actions, the dad held up his car keys and yelled, "The day my kids come back to any church will be the day my keys melt in hell!" Later the church members were shocked to learn that the dad had been struck dead in his backyard by lightning. His car keys were found in his pocket and had been melted by the lightning strike!

A person cannot offend the little ones (children) without offending the angel of the Lord assigned to guard over the children. The Herod who killed the infants in Bethlehem died in excruciating pain that was complicated by gangrene.

ANGELS WILL FIGHT AGAINST YOUR ENEMIES

The writer of Psalm 35 requested God to deliver him from those who persecuted him. While persecution is guaranteed in the life of a true believer, God will not allow the enemies of the faith to continue in their opposition against the gospel without His supernatural intervention. The psalmist requested:

> Let them be like chaff before the wind,
> And let the angel of the LORD chase them.
> Let their way be dark and slippery,
> And let the angel of the LORD pursue them.
>
> —PSALM 35:5–6

One of our personal friends and ministry missionaries, Kelvin McDaniel, has experienced God's protective hedge firsthand on numerous occasions. After returning from Indonesia several years ago, he shared this remarkable, firsthand account of God's angelic intervention on behalf of a church located in the midst of the largest Islamic population in the world. I quote from a letter sent to my office from missionary McDaniel:

> After years of terrorism against Christians in Indonesia, many of the wooden church structures have been burned down in the remote areas and islands. During a mission trip to Indonesia, I was asked by two dear Indonesian believers to preach at a remote church in West Java, which was one of the only wooden churches still standing, as every burnable structure (churches) within a one-hundred-mile radius had been burned to the ground.

After arriving on a Monday night, the small, white, wooden building, which could only hold two hundred people, was entirely packed. Giant speakers were set outside so the message could be heard in the Muslim communities over a mile in all directions. After the service, where souls were won to Christ, we piled in the vehicle and drove back to the city. At approximately five o'clock on Tuesday, after arriving at the airport, the translator's cell phone rang, and there was a desperate plea from the pastor of the small wooden church to speak with me to relate an astonishing event that had occurred.

That morning, a flatbed truck filled with Islamic terrorists arrived at the front door of the church. The pastor and his family live next door in a three-room apartment. The men began dragging a fifty-five-gallon oil drum filled with fuel, pouring it on the steps, and kicking in the door to pour it into the small church sanctuary. The fuel covered the floor, and the smell of gas filled the building. The pastor's wife ran out screaming for them not to burn the building down. She told them her children were in the apartment and this was the house of God. She then fell to her knees in the mixture of fuel, mud, and sod, begging them not to burn the house of God.

The fanatics began yelling that they were doing God's work by burning down the deceitful church. The leader slammed the now-empty barrel over the top of the stairs and into the building. The pastor's wife began pleading in prayer for the hand of the Lord to be with her and the family and the church building.

As the truck and the men pulled away to be out of danger's way, a lone man pulled out a box of matches. As he attempted to strike the match across the side of the box, nothing happened. He fumbled through the box, pulling out another match, only to have the same results. By this time hundreds had gathered to see the outcome of this assault on the Christian church. After several attempts, he suddenly shrieked out a terrible, blood-curdling scream and began running with his face frozen in a look of fear. He was grabbing his head and screaming with such passionate horror it seemed his mind had snapped.

Eventually, someone tackled him to prevent him from injuring himself and to assess his problem. He began throwing people off of him as they tried to hold him on the ground, scouring backward across the ground like a whipped animal. His eyes were wide open, and his face revealed sheer terror. Those who related the story said he was as afraid as a man being driven into the flames.

Eventually, he calmed down enough to tell with quivering lips what had occurred. As he told the story, between hard breaths, he would turn his head and shriek as if fearful of something attacking him from behind. He finally said that as he tried to light the final match and it fizzled out, an angel from God was standing directly in his face and said something so loudly to him that he thought the entire world must have heard it. Paralyzed momentarily in fear, he stared into the eyes of this messenger, which proclaimed, "I am a messenger of the Most High God sent to warn you so that you will warn others that this is God's real holy ground, and you will die if you do not flee."

As the pastor related this powerful story to me over the cell phone, I stood in the airport. I began crying, and as I was listening, I could hear the pastor say, "Brother, can you hear something? Do you hear the man yelling behind me now while we are talking?" I could faintly make out the voice of someone yelling in the far distance over the phone, but I was unable to make out his words. On the other end of the line, the pastor was holding his cell phone out in the air to pick up the voice of the man. He was yelling in his native language, and I was unable to interpret. The pastor told me it was the actual man who had that morning attempted to burn the church down. He was going from rooftop to rooftop and screaming his story to everyone, causing large numbers of salvations in the village yards and under trees! It reminded me of the verse in the Bible, "Let the angel of the Lord chase them."

This amazing story indicates that God is concerned for His people and will initiate a judgment against those who would harm His followers or destroy His church!

ANGELS ARE MOVED BY OUR PRAYERS

Then he said to me, "Do not fear, Daniel, for from the first day that you set your heart to understand, and to humble yourself before your God, your words were heard; and I have come because of your words. But the prince of the kingdom of Persia withstood me twenty-one days; and behold, Michael, one of the chief princes,

came to help me, for I had been left alone there with
the kings of Persia."

—DANIEL 10:12–13

The Scripture passage above refers to an amazing incident in
the life of the Hebrew prophet Daniel. This servant of God
was forced out of his homeland in Israel to serve the king
of Babylon during Israel's seventy years of captivity to King
Nebuchadnezzar and other kings of the Babylonian empire.
Under Daniel's watch, there were several prophetic dreams and
visions that were revealed to both the king and Daniel. On
one occasion, Daniel was unable to receive the understanding
to a strange and disturbing prophetic vision. This resulted in
a long, twenty-one-day fast and a season of prayer to beseech
God for a clear understanding of the unknown.

For three full weeks, Daniel fasted and prayed and was
unable to break through the heavens, which were like brass.
He was unaware that two opposing angels were engaged in
a cosmic conflict in the atmospheric heavens just above the
metropolis of Babylon. Eventually, God's messenger (many
believe it was Gabriel) called for reinforcements and was
assisted directly by the archangel Michael, who restrained a
spirit called the *prince of the kingdom of Persia*. This demonic
entity was what Paul later identified as a principality (Eph.
6:12), which is a chief ruling spirit that influences govern-
ments over nations, cities, or provinces.

The angel revealed that he had come to Daniel because
of his "words." These words were the prayers the prophet
had sent up to the heavenly temple, asking God to bring
the understanding. Gabriel is the chief angel that reveals
specific revelation from the throne of God and had previously

appeared twice to Daniel, giving the Hebrew prophet insight into prophetic events that would unfold in the future. (See Daniel 8:16; 9:21.) The Bible is clear that at times God sends answers to prayers through angels.

In the time of the second temple, there was a priest named Zacharias. His wife, Elizabeth, a cousin to Mary the mother of Christ, was an older woman and had never conceived. One morning while Zacharias was burning incense on the golden altar at the temple in Jerusalem, the angel Gabriel appeared on the right side of the altar with a message that Zacharias's wife, Elizabeth, would conceive and birth a son named *John*, who would come in the "spirit and power of Elijah" (Luke 1:4–17). Zacharias was frightened, perhaps because he was to be alone in the holy place when offering incense, and this *stranger* had entered, which could cause God's judgment to suddenly strike them both. Second, in Jewish tradition, the right side of the altar was reserved for God Himself. Perhaps Zacharias was fearful of dying if this was the Lord who was appearing! The angel announced, "Do not be afraid, Zacharias, for your prayer is heard" (Luke 1:13).

Here was a priest from the temple burning incense on the golden altar, which according to Scripture represents the prayers of the saints going up to God in His heavenly temple. The psalmist knew this when he wrote, "Let my prayer be set before You as incense, the lifting up of my hands as the evening sacrifice" (Ps. 141:2). How amazing that while Zacharias is presenting the prayer of others before God, the Lord answers his own prayer at the golden altar.

ANGELS GIVE HEED TO GOD'S WORD

Bless the LORD, you His angels,
Who excel in strength, who do His word,
Heeding the voice of His word.

—PSALM 103:20

Angels are assigned to perform the word or instructions God gives them. They are also interested in hearing the Word of God preached by mortal men. Peter wrote:

To them it was revealed that, not to themselves, but to us they were ministering the things which now have been reported to you through those who have preached the gospel to you by the Holy Spirit sent from heaven— things which angels desire to look into.

—1 PETER 1:12

JENTEZEN FRANKLIN AND ME

My wife and I have been close friends with Jentezen and Cherise Franklin for many years. I met Jentezen in Gastonia, North Carolina, in April 1982, shortly after my wife and I were married. In fact, I was married on Friday and began a three-week revival (called the *Honeymoon Revival* by the pastor of the church) on Sunday night! Jentezen and I became good friends, and on one occasion I asked him to accompany me to Romania. Communism had collapsed, and the nation was open to gospel meetings. I had spent time and money in preparation for this event.

When we arrived at the first city, someone had torn down all the posters, and there was great division among several of the churches. We went back to the hotel, and I was quite discouraged. It appeared that the entire group of meetings was going to be hindered and disrupted throughout the trip.

Besides this, the power in the city was being shut off at night. There was one small streetlight outside the hotel, and the room was pitch black. We stayed up in the dark, talking until about three in the morning. We both will never forget the moment that a *presence* came near the door of the room, and suddenly the entire room began to light up. We could see the pictures on the wall, the mirror, the chairs, and both beds. As this presence moved through the room and between the two beds, the hair on our arms rose up. We both began praying, crying, and rejoicing. This light in the room and the presence continued for about thirty minutes, and then it suddenly faded and left. We both expressed 100 percent confidence that an angel of the Lord was sent to strengthen and encourage us.

The next day we began traveling from city to city and ministering in large halls and centers—with overflow crowds attending each meeting. There were hundreds who came to Christ, and there was no hindrance during the entire trip. After numerous days of ministry, we both felt the presence eventually subside when we crossed the border from Romania to Hungary. To this day, we both believe that the Lord knew the opposition we two young ministers were experiencing, and as we asked God for His help, He sent a special messenger to go before us, just as the Lord had said to Moses, "Behold, My Angel shall go before you" (Exod. 32:34).

Chapter 7

FIVE THINGS THAT OFFEND THE ANGELS OF GOD

And do not grieve the Holy Spirit of God.

—EPHESIANS 4:30

WE ARE GOING TO TAKE A CLOSER LOOK AT OFFENSE in this chapter. We know from Ephesians 4:30 that it is possible to grieve the Holy Spirit.

Just as it is possible to grieve the Holy Spirit, it is also possible to grieve the Father. God was grieved by the wanderings and disobedience of the children of Israel as they journeyed toward the Promised Land. In Psalm 95 we are warned:

> Do not harden your hearts, as in the rebellion,
> As in the day of trial in the wilderness,
> When your fathers tested Me;
> They tried Me, though they saw My work.
> For forty years I was grieved with that generation,
> And said, "It is a people who go astray in their hearts,
> And they do not know My ways."
> So I swore in My wrath,
> "They shall not enter My rest."
>
> —PSALM 95:8–11

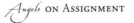

It is also possible to grieve the heart of Jesus. Several times in the New Testament, Jesus rebuked the disciples for their unbelief. He even wept at the tomb of Lazarus, not because Lazarus had died, but because He knew He was going to raise him from the dead. He wept because of the unbelief of the people around Him. (See John 11.)

Let's carry this a step further. If we can grieve the Holy Spirit, the Father, and Jesus Christ, then it is possible also to offend or grieve the angel of the Lord. In this chapter, we are going to not only find out that it is possible to do this, but we will also learn five things that grieve the angel of the Lord.

Angelic messengers are special messengers from God—appointed by God Himself. We learned earlier that the most common angels are called *ministering spirits* (Ps. 104:4). They go forth according to the purposes of God to complete a specific work, task, or assignment from the Lord.

What Happens When You Offend Your Angel?

Before we discuss the five things that can offend an angel, let's see what happens when an angel is offended. There is a story in the Bible that gives us a graphic look at this. In 1 Chronicles 21:1 we are told, "Now Satan stood up against Israel, and moved David to number Israel." David sent his commander, Joab, throughout the land to find out how many people they had.

In Exodus 30:11–12 we see that God had given clear instructions to Moses that whenever a census was taken of the people of Israel, every man in Israel was supposed to pay half a shekel unto the Lord as a ransom for his soul, or as the price of redemption. David numbered the people, but he did not pay the half shekel. David's disobedience angered God, so God sent a plague, and seventy thousand men died as a result of the plague (1 Chron. 21:14).

God sent an angel to destroy Jerusalem, the city of David, which is located on what is known today as Mount Moriah. When King David saw the destruction that God was bringing to Jerusalem, he realized that God was sending judgment because of his sin. As he looked up from where he stood on the slopes of Mount Moriah, he "saw the angel of the LORD standing between earth and heaven, having in his hand a drawn sword stretched out over Jerusalem" (1 Chron. 21:16). Immediately, David and all the elders clothed themselves in sackcloth and fell on their faces in repentance. The Lord "looked and relented of the disaster, and said to the angel who was destroying, 'It is enough; now restrain your hand'" (v. 15).

David ran to the top of the mountain and bought a threshing floor site from Ornan the Jebusite so that he could erect an altar to the Lord. We discover that Ornan had also seen the angel of the Lord, and in great fear he offered to give David everything he had—land and all. But David would not take it without paying full price for it.

It was there that David "built there an altar to the LORD, and offered burnt offerings and peace offerings, and called on the LORD; and He answered him from heaven by fire on the altar of burnt offering" (v. 26).

This is an example of a man willfully choosing to disobey God and of an angel becoming angry. That very mountain is the place where Abraham also built an altar and willingly offered to sacrifice his son, Isaac, in obedience to God. And, of course,

Mount Moriah is the place where Jesus, the Son of the living God, was crucified and paid the price of our redemption.

THE ANGEL OF THE LORD AS THE PREINCARNATE JESUS

There is a very important scripture about an angel in Exodus 23:

> Behold, I send an Angel before you to keep you in the way and to bring you into the place which I have prepared. Beware of Him and obey His voice; do not provoke Him, for He will not pardon your transgressions; for My name is in Him. But if you indeed obey His voice and do all that I speak, then I will be an enemy to your enemies and an adversary to your adversaries. For My Angel will go before you.
>
> —EXODUS 23:20–23

Here is the setting: The children of Israel were coming out of the bondage of Egypt and needed to know the direction they were to take in the wilderness. There were no road maps, signs, or GPS navigational systems to lead them. God had told them that He would not lead them through the land of the Philistines along the Sea: "'Lest perhaps the people change their minds when they see war, and return to Egypt.' So God led the people around by way of the wilderness of the Red Sea" (Exod. 13:17–18). Instead, God said that He would lead the people by way of the wilderness.

I used to get frustrated with the Israelites who complained and bickered so much during the years they spent wandering around the wilderness. But over the years, I've driven with many tour buses through that same wilderness, and believe me, I now understand. The heat pouring off the rocks and sand is intolerable; it truly is a "no-man's-land."

But God had already determined a way of leading them out and giving them direction. He was going to send an angel before them to keep them on the right path and to bring them to the land He had promised to them.

It is important to note that in Exodus 23:20 God said He was sending "an Angel" to guide them. A few verses later, God changes it to say, "My Angel" (v. 23). God gave one very unusual clue about this angel when He said, "My name is in Him" (v. 21). God had many names, including *El Shaddai*, *El-Elyon*, *Adonai*, and *El*, which is an Old Testament root name for *God* (Deut. 5:9). The two angels most recognized in the Bible are Gabriel and Michael—both names containing *el*, the name of God! In Exodus 6:3, God revealed Himself as *Yahweh*, appearing in Hebrew as four letters—*YHVH*—which is called the *tetragrammaton*. Many Jews still today will not try to pronounce that name because they consider it too sacred to speak aloud. When they write it, they often leave the word blank or write the name as "G-D."

This is a special angel, not a normal fighting prince or fighting angel. The Israelites were told, "Beware of Him and obey His voice; do not provoke Him, for He will not pardon your transgressions" (Exod. 23:21). This angel had to be something more than a regular angel. But it was not God, for only God can forgive sins, and this angel could not.

Many theologians believe that this angel was the preincarnate Jesus. Preincarnate simply means existence prior to His incarnation, or birth. There are several other places in the Old

Testament where Jesus is seen in His preincarnate state as the angel of the Lord.

- ▪ After Hagar became pregnant with Ishmael and was sent out away from the camp of Abraham, we see that "the Angel of the LORD found her by a spring of water in the wilderness, by the spring on the way to Shur" (Gen. 16:7).

- ▪ Later when Abraham sent Hagar and Ishmael away at the insistence of Sarah, Hagar went a short distance into the wilderness and fell to the ground, weeping about her situation. Then we see that "the angel of God called to Hagar out of heaven" and ministered to her, giving her a promise that God would make of Ishmael a great nation (Gen. 21:17–19).

- ▪ The angel of the Lord wrestled with Jacob (Gen. 32:24–30).

- ▪ The angel of the Lord spoke to Moses out of the burning bush (Exod. 3:1–14).

- ▪ The angel of the Lord stood in the way of Balaam and caused his donkey to speak (Num. 22:22–38).

- ▪ The angel of the Lord, as the captain of the host of the Lord, instructed Joshua to destroy Jericho (Josh. 5:13–6:5).

- ■ The angel of the Lord called Gideon to lead the Israelites against the Midianites (Judg. 6:11–24).

- ■ The angel of the Lord was the fourth man in the fire with Shadrach, Meshach, and Abednego (Dan. 3:28).

Was it Christ Himself who came down as the angel of the Lord? I believe that is more than likely. Usually when either Michael the archangel or Gabriel the messenger of God appeared in the Bible, they were named. (See Daniel 10:13; Luke 1:19, 26; Jude 9; Revelation 12:7.)

This angel who is instructed to lead the Israelites to the Promised Land is never mentioned by name. His name is secret. I believe that it was Jesus Christ in preincarnate form as the angel of the Lord who ministered to these Old Testament Bible characters. The "Angel of the Lord" never appears in the New Testament after the birth of Christ.

"Do Not Provoke Him"

The people of Israel were told not to provoke the angel of the Lord. If they did, they would be in serious trouble. *Provoke* means to grieve greatly or to vex a person. This is exactly what the Israelites did with their unbelief, bickering, and complaining. As a result, serious trouble came, and came swiftly.

1. They complained about the long walk through the wilderness:

Now when the people complained, it displeased the LORD; for the LORD heard it, and His anger was aroused. So the fire of the LORD burned among them, and consumed some in the outskirts of the camp. Then the people cried out to Moses, and when Moses prayed to the LORD, the fire was quenched. So he called the name of the place Taberah, because the fire of the LORD had burned among them.

—NUMBERS 11:1–3

2. They complained about Moses's Ethiopian wife:

Then Miriam and Aaron spoke against Moses because of the Ethiopian woman whom he had married; for he had married an Ethiopian woman.... So the anger of the LORD was aroused against them, and He departed. And when the cloud departed from above the tabernacle, suddenly Miriam became leprous, as white as snow.

—NUMBERS 12:1, 9–10

3. They complained about the giants in the land:

There we saw the giants (the descendants of Anak came from the giants); and we were like grasshoppers in our own sight, and so we were in their sight.

—NUMBERS 13:33

If this kind of complaining would grieve God in the Old Testament, I guarantee you that it will grieve God in the New Testament church of today. That's one of the things we have to be careful about.

Forty years after they left Egypt, the angel of the Lord had brought them to the edge of the Promised Land. As Joshua stood at the edge of the Promised Land, "a Man stood opposite him with His sword drawn in His hand" (Josh. 5:13). Joshua approached the man and asked, "Are You for us or for our adversaries?"

The man responded, "As captain of the host of the LORD am I now come" (v. 14, KJV). The Hebrew word used for "host" indicates a mass of people organized for war—an army. One of the names of God, used in Romans 9:29, is "The Lord of Sabaoth." It is the same word as *host* and is the name for an army. I believe that the captain of the host of the Lord standing before Joshua was none other than the angel of the Lord who had led Moses and the children of Israel through the wilderness for forty years. Now the cloud was gone, and the angel of the Lord, the preincarnate Christ, was prepared to lead Joshua and the people into the Promised Land.

FIVE THINGS THAT OFFEND THE ANGEL OF THE LORD

The children of Israel provoked the angel of the Lord to anger, or offended him by their actions over and over again on the journey to the Promised Land. As a result, they wandered for forty long, unnecessary years. Even after they took possession of the land, they continued to offend God with their actions, and as a result, they were repeatedly harassed, defeated, and taken captive by their enemies.

It is important to learn what offends the angels God has assigned to protect our lives and to direct us in the paths of the

Lord for our lives. There are five things that we can discover that will bring offense to the angels watching over us:

1. Negative words or wrong speaking will offend the angels.

Your negative words or wrong speaking can offend your angel. Psalm 103:20 says:

> Bless the LORD, you His angels,
> Who excel in strength, who do His word,
> Heeding the voice of His word.

The angels of the Lord are commissioned to listen to and be obedient to the voice of His Word. The Word of God moves the angels into action. First Peter 1:12 tells us that angels desire to look into the truth of the gospel and what it means. They crave knowledge about the preaching of the gospel and desire an understanding of God's Word about the blood of Jesus and its power to redeem mankind.

We learn in Hebrews 2:2 that "the word spoken through angels proved steadfast." God's Word tells us that the Law of God was given on Mount Sinai with ten thousand angels present (Deut. 33:2). The Word of God moves angels into action. I believe that in the same way, man's disobedience to the Word of God will offend the angels and cause them to withhold their protection.

In the time of Israel's release from the bondage of Egypt, Pharaoh was judged by how he treated the Israelite people. He came against the word of God given to him by Moses, and as a result, plagues were released against Egypt.

When the Hebrew people began to speak against God

in the wilderness, difficulties began to rise against them, including plagues and disease. The Bible records the number of plagues:

1. They began to misuse their tongue, and fire came into the camp and destroyed them (Num. 11:1).

2. When the people began to lust after the rich foods they had eaten in Egypt and complained and wept for meat to eat, the Lord sent quail. But as judgment for their disobedience and misuse of their tongues, sickness immediately fell upon them from eating the quail (Num. 11:4–35).

3. When Miriam and Aaron misused their tongues to complain about the Ethiopian woman Moses had married, the anger of the Lord was kindled against them, and a plague of leprosy came upon Miriam (Num. 12:1–16).

4. When the ten spies returned with reports of "giants in the land" too powerful to overcome, the people began complaining against Moses and the Lord for bringing them to a land filled with enemies, and they wanted to choose another leader. However, Caleb and Joshua reported that they were well able to overcome, and begged them to stop their complaining

and to trust God's leading. The people wanted to stone Caleb and Joshua instead. As a result, God told Moses that the entire generation who complained would die without ever being allowed to enter the Promised Land (Num. 13:31–33; 14:1–35).

5. When Korah and his company of men challenged the authority and leadership of Moses and Aaron and tried to assume spiritual leadership of the children of Israel, God became angry and caused an earthquake to open the ground under the tents of Korah and all his followers, and they were destroyed in the pit (Num. 16:1–40).

6. The day after God destroyed Korah and his company, the people of Israel again complained to Moses, saying that he had killed the people of the Lord. In anger, God caused a plague to immediately begin to kill off the Israelites. Moses and Aaron quickly began to intercede for the people and wave an offering of incense over the people to God, and in response, God stopped the plague—but 14,700 people died as a result of the judgment of God (Num. 16:41–50).

7. After a great victory over the Canaanites, the people began a journey through Edom

and again complained to Moses and God
for having to travel in the heat of the desert
without their favorite foods. As a result, God
sent serpents to bite the people. In response,
God directed Moses to erect the bronze
serpent, which would protect the people if they
looked upon it (Num. 21:5–9).

8. When the people of Israel began to commit
adultery with the women of Moab and began
to worship their gods, God again sent a plague
that destroyed twenty-four thousand Israelites
(Num. 25:1–9).

The Israelite people were in a mess! Eight times they brought on the wrath of God because of their murmuring and complaining and disobedience. What a powerful illustration of the truth that the power of life and death is in the tongue (Prov. 18:21).

Remember that when the children of Israel began their journey to the Promised Land, the Lord said an angel would go before them. God warned the people not to offend this angel of the Lord because if they did, the angel would stop them from inheriting the land. (See Exodus 23:20–21 and Judges 2:1–4.) For a moment, think about how many people of God today fall into the trap of complaining about a ministry, a preacher, or other Christians, and as a result, the blessings of God are withheld in their lives or in their church.

Let me tell you of one example from my father's ministry. My father pastored a church in Bailey's Crossroads, Virginia, which he grew from ten members to more than one hundred twenty-five. In the early days of his ministry there, Dad had to work at another job part-time, and Mom had to work also because the church could not adequately support them. During that time, there was a man who served on the pastor's council.

The time came when the church was able to give Dad a salary. When that happened, this man on the council began to complain about the need to pay my dad a salary. One day while this man was at home, as he stood near an open window, all of a sudden two hands struck him between the shoulders and knocked him down. His head hit the radiator and knocked out his front teeth.

Because there was no one in the house but this man and his wife, at first he thought it must have been his wife! However, she was busy sewing in another room. He had to go to the hospital and get stitches. He was very frightened because he realized actual physical hands had struck him.

Let me help you understand what I believe happened to this man by giving an example from God's Word. In Luke 16:19–31 we have the story of the rich man in hell who pleaded with Abraham to allow Lazarus to "dip the tip of his finger in water and cool my tongue; for I am tormented in this flame" (v. 24). I've always wanted to know why he would say his tongue was tormented. Well, if you will go to the story, you will see that before the rich man went to hell, a poor man was sitting at the foot of his table trying to catch the crumbs that fell while the rich man ate. The very thing that represented what he used to withhold help to this poor man—his mouth eating food—was the thing that God judged to burn throughout eternity. He could have used his mouth to help someone else, and he didn't.

Perhaps if he had refused to give money to the poor man, the back of his hip would have burned because of his greed.

In another example from my dad's ministry, a woman in his church created contention during a business meeting. While my dad was speaking, this woman stood up and started shouting, "Come out of him, you devil!"

At first my dad thought it must be a CB radio system and turned around to see this woman standing up. He asked, "Who are you talking to, woman?"

She said, "I'm talking to you."

"Who are you calling a devil?" he asked.

She said, "I'm calling you a devil."

My dad's left hand began to shake under the power of God. He began to pray in tongues and rebuke the spirit of the enemy. As a result, this woman walked out of the church.

The next day that woman could not speak at all. She remained unable to speak for nearly a year. She went to the doctor, and the doctor said, "There is no explanation for this. We cannot find anything wrong with your vocal cords. You have simply gone totally dumb." He told her it would cost her thousands of dollars to travel to New Orleans to see a specialist and try to find out what happened to her voice. Her condition continued for several more months.

Then one day the Lord spoke to my dad and said, "Now, Fred, this woman is not going to repent. She is proud and is not going to repent for what she said to you. But her children need her. I will heal her if you are willing to stand in the gap and tell her that you release her and forgive her."

Shortly after this, while I was in revival there, the woman attended the service. When my dad saw her, he asked her to come up to the front. He also called my mother to the front. Quietly, he told her that because she was proud and would not repent, she had not been healed yet. But God had told him that if he and my mother would forgive her and stand in the gap for her, God would heal her. My dad and mother assured her that they had forgiven her.

The next morning at six o'clock, the woman was totally healed. However, she never repented, if you can believe that. Her house burned down twice. She and her husband had marital problems. Recently my dad found out that she had been killed in a horrific car accident. I believe the woman would not have suffered the way she did if she had not offended the Holy Spirit by offending my father.

Because my dad forgave her and released her in the spirit realm, she was healed. He understands the spiritual realm and does not walk in bitterness and unforgiveness. But she had also offended the Holy Spirit. And because you should not offend the Holy Spirit, God allowed a very swift judgment to come to her.

2. Unbelief will offend the angels.

Let me give you another example from God's Word of how the angel of the Lord can bring judgment upon you. In Luke 1:8–20, Zacharias the priest was about to administer prayers upon the golden altar. As he walked into the holy of holies before the altar, he saw an angel standing at the right side of the altar. (See Luke 1:5–23.) Tradition says that if the priest saw an angel of the Lord on the right side of the altar, it meant that God had come down. It was a very serious moment, and the priest could be struck dead by the presence of God. Zacharias was filled with fear. No one else was permitted to come in, so he knew it was not another priest.

The angel said to him, "You are going to have a son. He is going to be named John. He is going to go before the Lord and is going to come in the spirit of Elijah." (See Luke 1:13–17.)

Now, that is very detailed information. Zacharias should have praised God and said, "Thank You for coming. We have been praying for a family." But does he say that? No, he says, "How shall I know that? Give me a sign." (See verse 18.)

The angel of the Lord was offended, and he said, "You will be mute and not able to speak until the day these things take place, because you did not believe my words" (v. 20). Unbelief can offend an angel of God.

How different is the story of Mary in Luke 1:26–38! An angel appeared to Mary and said, "And behold, you will conceive in your womb and bring forth a Son, and shall call His name Jesus. He will be great, and will be called the Son of the Highest" (vv. 31–32). Once again, an angel appears to tell Mary she will have a boy named Jesus, and he tells her His destiny and purpose. Now, if anyone should have doubted, Mary should have doubted. She was just a young girl, possibly fourteen or fifteen, and not even married. She should be the one to say, "Look, maybe You have the wrong house. I'm not even married."

Instead, she said to the angel, "Let it be to me according to your word" (v. 38). That is faith. She was honored as a woman of great faith because she believed what the angel told her.

It is clear that unbelief can offend the angel of God. That is the whole story of the children of Israel. If you will read Exodus and Numbers, you will see that the nation of Israel offended the angel of the Lord over and over again. Zacharias, a priest of God, should have believed the angel's words and not doubted. Yet he doubted. But Mary, a young virgin girl, heard a message that seemed impossible, but she believed.

God does not honor unbelief. For God to honor our unbelief would be totally contrary to the law of faith, for the Bible says, "Without faith it is impossible to please [God]" (Heb. 11:6). The Bible says that it was the unbelief of the people of Nazareth that prevented Jesus from being able to do mighty works in that city—His hometown (Matt. 13:58). In Matthew 17:20, the disciples were unable to cast evil spirits out of a little boy, and Jesus gave only one reason—because of their unbelief. He said, "This kind does not go out except by prayer and fasting" (v. 21). That could mean this kind of evil spirit or this kind of unbelief—the only way you could get rid of your unbelief was by prayer and fasting. God does not honor unbelief. Unbelief can literally stop the blessings of God.

Unbelief can offend the angel of God. Unbelief can hinder healing; unbelief can stop the blessings of God in general. We must be careful what we say and how we say it.

3. Sin will offend your angel.

In John 5:1–15 we find the story of the lame man who had been lying at the pool of Bethesda for thirty-eight years, waiting to be the first in the water when the angel came and stirred the waters. When Jesus saw him lying there, He immediately told him, "Rise, take up your bed and walk" (v. 8). The man was immediately healed. Jesus then said to him, "See, you have been made well. Sin no more, lest a worse thing come upon you" (v. 14). A person can be forgiven and set free of a sin, but if they go back into sin, it will open the door for that particular sin to come back upon them.

When we speak of sin, we think of adultery, fornication, lying, murder, stealing, and so forth. But remember that offending with your words—complaining, criticizing, and speaking negative things of the Spirit of God—is also a sin, and you will be judged accordingly.

At one time I was preaching a revival that continued for three weeks. One night a man came up to me whom I had seen in the services night after night. He always quoted a scripture to me when I spoke with him, and I thought this man must be a man of faith. He said to me, "Preacher, I want you to pray for me. I'm going deaf in both ears."

I asked, "Why are you going deaf? Can they tell you why you are going deaf?"

"Nope," he answered, "they can't tell me why I'm going deaf. But I want a miracle." He started quoting healing scriptures to me.

So I put my fingers in his ears and started to pray. As I began, the Holy Spirit said to me, "Get your fingers out of his ears. He has offended Me." I thought, "What in the world?" Why had the Lord stopped me? I thought, "Let me try this again," and I tried the spirits to see what was going on.

The Lord spoke to me again in my spirit. "This man has complained about the music in this church and about the choruses they sing, and he has offended Me. Since he doesn't like the music, I'm going to let him go deaf so he won't hear it anymore and complain." I told the man what the Lord had told me.

He protested and tried to say, "I don't know anything about that."

I told him, "Don't you lie to the Holy Spirit. You've spoken evil about some of the music of this church." This made him mad, and he went back and sat down and folded his arms.

After the service, I told the pastor what had happened. He said, "You said what? You told the man that?"

"Yes, I did," I answered. "I told the man what the Spirit of God had said to me."

The pastor said, "But I hadn't told you anything about that man."

I said, "No, you didn't. But was I in order? If I wasn't in order, I'm going to apologize to the man."

Then the pastor told me, "When I brought my new music director in, that man would sit on the front row and put cotton in his ears. The cotton would hang down all the way to his neck. And he would stand up, face the church, and show them that he didn't like the music."

> WE CAN BIND THE PRESENCE OF GOD, BIND THE PROTECTION FROM THE ANGEL OF GOD, BY THE VERY THINGS THAT WE SAY OR DO.

I said, "Let me tell you something, Pastor. The Lord spoke to me and told me he had offended the church and the pastor, and as a result, he wouldn't get healed."

Here is the good thing you can learn from this story. The Lord gives you an opportunity to repent and come clean with your sin. But that man never came back and apologized. He never owned up to his spiritual pride and would not believe that it was the Holy Spirit at work in his life.

One time when I was preaching a revival, my brother and his wife told me the story of a man in their church. I was teaching on worship. One of the verses in the Bible that I used speaks about dancing before the Lord. I explained what that meant. There was an old man in the church who loved the Lord but didn't believe in dancing before the Lord. Like many other people, he was a good man doing everything right in many areas but still missing the point in just one area—and it was costing him.

This old man said, "I don't believe all that. When people get up and jump up and down, that is all of the devil. God don't do things like that."

Immediately following that statement, he began experiencing pains in his feet and below his ankles. Eventually, he had to have his toes and part of his foot amputated. He got to the point that he couldn't walk, couldn't stand up and shout if he wanted to, because of the condition of his feet.

It's not that God is out there trying to judge everybody and inflict them with disease and judgment. We can go back to the children of Israel to understand this principle. When the Israelites offended the angel of God, God took down the hedge of protection from around them, and they began to be attacked by their enemies. When we offend the angel of the Lord, the same thing happens. When we offend the Holy Spirit or the angel of God, then He cannot defend us and bring us healing as in the story of the man at the pool of Bethesda. He cannot step in and intervene in our situation.

We can bind the presence of God, bind the protection from the angel of God, by the very things that we say or do.

Sin will offend the angel of God.

4. Not giving God the glory can offend the angel of the Lord.

This story is told in Acts 12:1–2, 20–25, of King Herod, who killed James, a wonderful apostle of Christ. When he saw how pleased the Jews were by this act, he imprisoned Peter and planned to kill him also. However, due to the protection of his own angel, Peter escaped from prison.

Shortly after this, King Herod appeared before all the people dressed in regal garments and sitting upon a throne. Josephus describes Herod as dressed in a garment covered with silver from his neck down. When the sun hit the silver of his garment, it glowed, and the people began to shout, saying, "[It's] the voice of a god and not of a man!" (v. 22). Herod did nothing to stop the shouts of the people, and the Bible says, "Then immediately an angel of the Lord struck him, because he did not give glory to God. And he was eaten by worms and died" (v. 23).

Understand what this is saying: Herod wasn't killed because he killed James or because he arrested Peter. He was struck down by the Lord because "he did not give glory to God." In *Antiquities of the Jews*, book 19, chapter 8, section 2, Josephus expands on this story by giving more details about what happened to Herod, saying that he fell into the deepest of sorrows, a severe pain arose in his bowels, and he died after the eighth day.

An angel of the Lord smote Herod. I believe the angel

that released Peter from prison was likely the same angel that brought judgment to Herod.

Not giving God the glory can bring offense to the angel of God.

5. Disobedience to the Word can offend your angel.

In Numbers 22 we find the story of Balaam. He was a seer and a great prophet who had great power. He could prophesy things that were going to come to pass. In this chapter, messengers of Moab came to Balaam, and they said, "Look, we'll pay any amount of money you want to stand on the mountain and curse these people." Two times God admonished Balaam not to go with the men and do as they asked. The third time they asked, Balaam went with them. As he was riding on his donkey, an angel appeared in front of the donkey. The Lord opened the donkey's eyes to see the angel, and in fear the donkey stepped aside and, in doing so, crushed Balaam's foot against the wall. In anger, Balaam began beating the donkey.

The angel began to speak through the donkey's mouth to Balaam—almost like a ventriloquist would speak through his puppet. Now, if a donkey began talking to me and rebuking me, I'd jump off that donkey, go home, call Barnum and Bailey circus, and say, "Look I've got a talking donkey. I mean, the dude talks!" Who is going to start fussing with a donkey? But Balaam got off the donkey and started fussing and arguing with the donkey.

Finally, the angel of the Lord heard and severely rebuked Balaam, saying, "Why have you struck your donkey these three times? Behold, I have come out to stand against you, because your way is perverse before Me. The donkey saw Me and turned aside from Me these three times. If she had not turned aside from Me, surely I would also have killed you by now, and let her live" (vv. 32–33).

The angel of the Lord stood there in front of the donkey to resist the blessing of Balaam, to resist the prophecies of Balaam, because he had a very perverse way. There was something about him that just was not right.

ANYONE CAN OFFEND AN ANGEL

Let me make this point: good people who love the Lord can still offend their angels in some of the five ways I've listed.

Moses was the meekest man in all the earth. Moses is listed among the Jewish people as being one of the greatest men who ever lived, along with Elijah. Yet Moses offended the angel of the Lord even after God told him not to.

In the story of Moses leading the people to the Promised Land, after they had been wandering in the wilderness for a very long time—thirty-eight years—the people were still complaining. They said to Moses, "Why have you brought up the assembly of the LORD into this wilderness, that we and our animals should die here?...It is not a place of grain or figs or vines or pomegranates; nor is there any water to drink" (Num. 20:4–5). Moses and Aaron left the complaining people, went into the tabernacle, and fell on their faces before the Lord, asking His help once again. God responded to their prayer and told them, "Take the rod; you and your brother Aaron gather the congregation together. Speak to the rock before their eyes, and it will yield its water; thus you shall bring water for them out of the rock, and give drink to the congregation and their animals" (v. 8).

I've heard many preachers say that the reason Moses was not allowed to go into the Promised Land was because he struck the rock two times instead of merely speaking to it as the Lord had instructed him. I believed that was true until I traveled to the country of Jordan and heard our Christian Arab tour guide give his explanation.

He took us to Numbers 20:10, where Moses and Aaron were aggravated with the people. They were always complaining, they were always negative, and now they wanted water from the rock. Moses said, "Hear now, you rebels! Must we bring water for you out of this rock?" After thirty-eight long years in the wilderness, Moses was growing pretty frustrated with the complaints of the people. In verse 11, Moses hits the rock two times instead of speaking to it.

Because of his disobedience, God tells Moses, "Because you did not believe Me, to hallow Me in the eyes of the children of Israel, therefore you shall not bring this assembly into the land which I have given them" (v. 12). It is right after this incident that Aaron, the high priest, dies (vv. 24–26).

I now believe that the reason God told Moses, "You are going to die short of the Promised Land, and you are not going to be able to enter the Promised Land" was just as God states in verse 12: Moses did not "hallow Me in the eyes of the children of Israel." In other words, Moses did not tell the people it would be the Lord who brought water out of the rock. He did not give the glory to God, saying instead, "Must we bring water for you out of this rock?"

I believe that at times there are people who do not receive

the things they need from the Lord because their motives for receiving these things are not right. Someone may say, "O God, I want You to bless me, and if You do, I will be a giver." But they aren't already givers and don't really intend to become a giver if God blesses them. Others may not receive from the Lord because He knows they do not intend to give Him the glory.

WHAT TO DO IF YOU HAVE OFFENDED THE ANGEL OF THE LORD

There are three things you should do if you feel that somehow you have really offended God:

1. *Confess your sin.* Pray, "Lord, I have really done wrong." Don't wait for someone to come to you and ask you to forgive them. Confess your sin before God.

2. *Repent.* Repent means more than merely confessing your sin. Repent means to turn. Tell the Lord that with His help you are not going to do the things that offended Him anymore. Turn from your sin, and commit to do your best to walk with Him daily.

3. *Ask God to help you to forgive others who have wronged you, and find a way to restitution with that person.* In other words, write a letter to that person if you cannot physically see him or her. Tell them that although the situation

may have happened years earlier, you have
asked God to forgive you for your unforgiving
spirit, and now you are asking that person to
forgive you. This is an extremely important
step to take, especially if you need a healing.

I recently heard a young man in Cleveland, Tennessee, give a
testimony. He had been in a wheelchair for many years. Many
people had prayed for him, but he had not been healed. He
said this: "I finally got into a meeting where the power of God
was moving." He said that he simply humbled himself before
God. He quit being bitter with God. He quit asking God why
he wasn't healed. The power of God hit him, and he got out
of that wheelchair and walked. The key was that he humbled
himself before God. You can never go wrong by humbling
yourself before God and saying, "Lord, I need Your help." God
will honor your faith; He will honor your integrity.

If we walk faithfully with God, all of God's presence, all of
God's power, and all of the blessings of God will be ours.

Chapter 8

DAVID'S UNDERSTANDING
OF THE MIZPAH MARKER

And David stayed in strongholds in the
wilderness, and remained in the mountains in
the Wilderness of Ziph. Saul sought him every
day, but God did not deliver him into his hand.

—1 SAMUEL 23:14

THERE IS NO SHORTAGE OF ROCKS AND STONES IN
Israel. From the rolling limestone hills of Jerusalem to the
dull, rose-colored jagged mountains of the Judean wilderness,
rocks are everywhere. In Israel's early history, when patriarchs
and prophets received a visitation of God or an angel at a
certain location, they would erect either an altar or a monument of stone. Leaders like Abraham and Jacob built altars
and offered sacrificial gifts to God for His favor, promises, and
blessings (Gen. 22:9; 35:1). Others, like Joshua, laid piles of
stones or erected large, rock monuments as visible markers of
God's promise to Israel (Josh. 4:6; 24:27). The purpose of the
stone altar or monument was to create a visual monument that
future generations could look at and be reminded of God's

promises and His visitations to His chosen people, the Israelites. Every Hebrew understood the power of the monument and how it marked the spot. They also knew that the eyes of the Lord were always on this *spot* and were reminded of His covenant with His people.

From the moment Jacob piled the stones on the land near Mizpah, the location became known as a special place where God would help His people and protect them from danger. In the time of Samuel, the people were under the oppression of the Philistines for twenty years (1 Sam. 7:2). The prophet Samuel instructed the people to put away all idolatry and to prepare their hearts for the Lord to intervene on their behalf (1 Sam. 7:3). We read:

> And Samuel said, "Gather all Israel to Mizpah, and I will pray to the LORD for you." So they gathered together at Mizpah, drew water, and poured it out before the Lord. And they fasted that day, and said there, "We have sinned against the LORD." And Samuel judged the children of Israel at Mizpah.
>
> —1 SAMUEL 7:5–6

All of Israel gathered at Mizpah, the place where the protective covenant was forged between Laban and Jacob. As they poured out the drink offering, offered a lamb, and cried out unto the Lord, He sent a great thunder and frightened their enemies (1 Sam. 7:10). Again, a special monument was placed at the site of God's intervention:

> Then Samuel took a stone and set it up between Mizpah and Shen, and called its name Ebenezer, saying, "Thus far the LORD has helped us." So the Philistines were subdued,

and they did not come anymore into the territory of Israel. And the hand of the LORD was against the Philistines all the days of Samuel.

—1 SAMUEL 7:12–13

DAVID PROTECTS HIS FAMILY

Samuel was the prophet who anointed David to be the future king of Israel (1 Sam. 16:13). After slaying Goliath, David married King Saul's daughter Michal and became a national hero in the eyes of Israel. Women began singing songs about David (1 Sam. 18:7–9), which infuriated Saul. From that moment, the jealous king opened a spiritual door for a tormenting spirit that motivated the king to assassinate David. The mad king would throw javelins at David and make threats against his own family members for favoring David. This mental insanity drove Saul to direct a slaughter of eighty-five priests of God who were living at the tabernacle in Nob (1 Sam. 22:13–19).

David and six hundred mighty men became fugitives, living from cave to cave in the hot Judean wilderness. David was unable to see his wife and was fearful of visiting his family in Bethlehem because Saul was familiar with David's family and his hometown. Eventually, David made a decision to get his family to a place of security and protection:

> David therefore departed from there and escaped to the cave of Adullam. And when his brothers and all his father's house heard it, they went down there to him. And everyone who was in distress, everyone who was in debt, and everyone who was discontented gathered to

> him. So he became captain over them. And there were about four hundred men with him. Then David went from there to Mizpah of Moab; and he said to the king of Moab, "Please let my father and mother come here with you, till I know what God will do for me."
>
> —1 Samuel 22:1–3

The king of Moab received David's family, and, although David and his family and his men and their families moved several additional times while David was running from Saul, they remained hidden and safe from Saul's anger for the rest of Saul's life. It was obvious that the Lord had departed from Saul and had transferred the mantle of blessing to David, the future king of Israel (1 Sam. 16:14).

> And David stayed in strongholds in the wilderness, and remained in the mountains in the Wilderness of Ziph. Saul sought him every day, but God did not deliver him into his hand.
>
> —1 Samuel 23:14

It is rather difficult to explain today why marking a location was significant and why godly men would often return to that same area in the future when they needed to hear from the Lord, renew a covenant, or experience a fresh visitation. However, God was certainly familiar with the importance of locations. When He spoke to Abraham to offer Isaac on the altar, He said, "Go to the land of Moriah, and offer him there as a burnt offering on one of the mountains of which I shall tell you" (Gen 22:2). God had selected a specific mountain in a certain location for an important reason.

THE MARKING OF MOUNT MORIAH

To understand the significance of the phrase "one of the mountains of which I shall tell you," we must first understand the location and prophetic importance of Mount Moriah. The story actually begins in Genesis 14. Five foreign kings had invaded the cities of the plain and taken the people and goods into their control (Gen. 14:1–2). Abraham organized an army of 318 of his personal servants and chased down and defeated these five kings. In appreciation, Abraham, along with the king of Sodom, brought the people and their possessions to Jerusalem, where he met with the mysterious first king-priest, Melchizedek. We read:

> Then Melchizedek king of Salem brought out bread and wine; he was the priest of God Most High. And he blessed him and said: "Blessed be Abram of God Most High, possessor of heaven and earth; and blessed be God Most High, who has delivered your enemies into your hand." And he gave him a tithe of all.
>
> —GENESIS 14:18–20

Jewish rabbis and Christian scholars agree that this event occurred in Jerusalem (then called the city of Salem—Gen. 14:18) in the Valley of Shaveh, known as the King's Valley (Gen. 14:17). Today, this valley is called *the Kidron Valley* and is the ravine that lies between the Eastern Gate in Jerusalem and the Mount of Olives. I have personally seen an archeological excavation that is presently taking place at the lower edge of the Kidron Valley, near the ancient ruins of the Pool of Siloam in Jerusalem. The archeologist personally told me that he had unearthed tunnels and a water channel that dates back to the time of Abraham and Melchizedek, one of the earliest known levels of Jerusalem's occupation. The mountain just above the Kidron Valley is known as *Mount Moriah.* Thus, Abraham presented the tithe (the tenth) to the Lord in the land of Moriah.

> LIKE DAVID, WHO MOVED HIS FAMILY TO A PLACE OF PROTECTION AT MIZPAH, YOU TOO CAN MAKE A DECISION TO GET YOUR FAMILY TO A PLACE OF SECURITY AND PROTECTION THROUGH THE MIZPAH COVENANT.

Many years later, God called Abraham back to this same location and requested that he place his covenant son, Isaac, on the altar. God instructed, "Take now your son, your only son Isaac, whom you love, and go to the land of Moriah, and offer him there as a burnt offering on one of the mountains of which I shall tell you" (Gen. 22:2). Abraham returned to the very land where he had met the first king and priest, Melchizedek. God knew that His Son would one day live on Earth as a man and be offered in Jerusalem on one of the mountains in the land of Moriah. Paul tells us that Christ is a High Priest "according to the order of Melchizedek" (Heb. 5:10).

The imagery in Genesis 22 is a preview and a prophetic pattern of what would one day occur in Jerusalem. The loving father Abraham was offering his covenant son, Isaac, on the altar of Moriah in Jerusalem, just as the heavenly Father would one day give His Son on the cross in Jerusalem.

- Abraham offered his "only son,"—and Christ was God's "only begotten son."
- Abraham saw the place on the third day—and Christ was seen alive after the third day.
- Abraham predicted that Isaac would return off the altar—as Christ predicted He would rise again.
- Abraham laid the sacrificial wood upon Isaac to carry—and Christ carried the cross and our sins.
- Abraham said God would provide a lamb—and Christ was the final "lamb of God" for sins.
- Abraham predicted it would be seen in the mount of the Lord—and Christ was seen in the mount.

This famous event recorded in Genesis 22, and the fact that Mount Moriah was to be the location of the final sin offering through Christ, was why God inspired Solomon to construct the temple on Mount Moriah.

> Now Solomon began to build the house of the LORD at Jerusalem on Mount Moriah, where the LORD had appeared to his father David, at the place that David had prepared on the threshing floor of Ornan the Jebusite.
> —2 CHRONICLES 3:1

This mountain became a sacred marker and a spiritual boundary because of an event in the life of Abraham, which became a prophetic preview of the final act of redemption that would unfold in A.D. 32 near the Jewish temple in Jerusalem.

BACK TO MIZPAH

Certainly David, who understood the importance of places of visitation, and who had read the Torah (the first five books of the Bible), knew the story of Jacob's Mizpah covenant as part of Israel's spiritual history. David was, no doubt, concerned that since Saul was unable to personally harm him, the angry king would ride into Bethlehem and slaughter his family members. David's six hundred men were riding horses from cave to cave, to and from strongholds throughout the desert. Since Saul was in control of all of Israel, any hideaway inside the nation would have been an open road for Saul and his cronies. The coastal areas were controlled by the Philistines, who were Israel's enemies. The best choice for David's family was across the Jordan River in an area that bore the same name as the covenant that Jacob and Laban initiated.

During Saul's reign and throughout the time when David was a wanted man, neither he nor his family members perished. The king-elect understood that his family and he were living under the continual threat of danger. The ancient Hebrews understood the power of covenants and that God's attention was always drawn to the covenant and the place where the covenant was ratified. This is why men would return to the altars and pillars in time of need and renew their spiritual vision and seek the attention and favor of God. David knew the covenant of protection at Mizpah and sent his closest loved ones to the mountain.

The protective angels were still at work.

Chapter 9

ANGELS AND THE
MIZPAH COVENANT

Do not forget to entertain strangers, for by so
doing some have unwittingly entertained angels.

—HEBREWS 13:2

As NOTED EARLIER, JACOB SAW THE ANGELS OF THE LORD immediately after Laban and he sealed the Mizpah covenant, and later as he wrestled a man who was an angel in human form. (See Hebrews 13:2.) The heavenly host is fully aware of the covenants that the Almighty has made with His people, including the covenants of Noah, Abraham, David, and the new covenant through Christ.

All believers who have received Christ as their Lord and Savior have a redemptive covenant through the shed blood of the Redeemer (Eph. 1:7). Part of our covenant includes God's hand of protection upon our lives. This protection is often provided by angels of the Lord. The Book of Job tells the story of a wealthy Middle Eastern businessman named Job, who was the wealthiest man in the East. According to Job 1:1–4, his portfolio included:

- Seven thousand sheep
- Three thousand camels
- Five hundred yoke of oxen
- Five hundred female donkeys
- Ten children
- Homes

Satan, the adversary, was attempting to invade Job's property but was unable to do so due to a "hedge" of protection that surrounded Job, his livestock, and his family. Satan requested God to remove the hedge from Job and allow his animals and children to be attacked (Job 1:9–10). Both God and Satan knew an invisible hedge protected Job, but Job himself was unaware of this invisible protective hedge. This lends to the theory that the hedge was an encampment of angels that surrounded God's man Job. Angels could be seen by both God and Satan but not by Job. Since Job loved and feared God, he was a candidate for the protection spoken of in Psalm 34:7:

> The angel of the LORD encamps all around those who
>   fear Him,
> And delivers them.

ANGELS FORM PROTECTIVE CIRCLES AROUND THE RIGHTEOUS. A SINGLE ANGEL CAN PROVIDE BETTER PROTECTION THAN THE ENTIRE SECRET SERVICE!

Angels form protective circles around the righteous. The prophet Elisha enjoyed supernatural protection from his enemies as the "horses and chariots of fire" encircled his servant and him (2 Kings 6:17). The angel who spoke to the prophet Zechariah revealed God's plan for the restoration of Jerusalem. The Almighty announced that He would be a "wall of fire all around" the city (Zech. 2:5). A single angel can provide better protection than the entire Secret Service!

A COVENANT WITH GOD

I grew up with what has been termed a "classical Full Gospel background." I can recall that we were raised with very strict standards, especially when it came to what was termed "outward adornment." Women did not cut their hair or wear makeup or any form of jewelry. Although our church members were considered *odd* by Christians from other denominations, by and large the people were very humble, simple, and very dedicated to the Lord. They would often make a *vow* to God, and this vow would become a part of their daily walk with the Lord.

A noted minister with the last name Carroll made one such vow. From the beginning of his ministry, he told God that if God would take care of his family, he (the minister) would always take care of God's business. Reverend Carroll trusted God completely to provide for his family and himself, and in return, he dedicated his entire life each day to the work of the Lord.

Brother Carroll served his denomination (the Church of God) as an assistant state overseer. Because the head bishop was sick, Reverend Carroll was called upon to go out of town for a conference. He got into the automobile and started it to get ready to make the trip. He was unaware that his five-year-old son, Jack, had been playing behind the car, smelled the fumes when the car was started, and passed out. As Reverend Carroll backed up the car, he accidently ran over Jack. When he jumped out of the car, he saw that his little son's head had been run over and his eyes were protruding out of his head. He picked him up, took him into the house, and laid him on the bed. Everyone was upset and crying out in prayer.

The preacher said and did something that his daughter Ruth would never forget. He told his wife, "The Lord has told me that if I'd take care of His business, then He would take care of mine!" Then he got into his car and headed to the conference. He was so dedicated to the church and the work of God that he trusted God to heal his son. Ruth was a young girl, and she recalled her mother and all the children praying. She said, "Jack's face was swollen and in horrible condition and was all out of proportion. He was completely unconscious."

Later, Ruth said that at the very moment the minister returned home and drove his car into the driveway, "It looked like someone stuck a pin in Jack's head. His face began to go down. His eye and ear went back into place. It was amazing to watch. Jack looked up at his mother and said, 'You know, I missed supper—I'm hungry.' He was instantly healed, just like nothing ever happened. Jack had no side effects or scars to show that the accident ever happened. Dad always believed that if you asked God for anything (especially miracles pertaining to sickness), God would always supernaturally come through."

I personally knew Jack Carroll. He served as our ministry's certified public accountant from the early beginnings in the 1980s until his death. His sister Ruth was one of the first people Pam and I met before moving to Cleveland, and her husband, Ralph, has served from the beginning on our ministry board of directors. I recall hearing this story many years ago, and I believe God honored the vow of this man of God, promising him, "If you will take care of My family, I will always take care of your business."

This is very similar to the Mizpah covenant. This covenant asks God to watch over your loved ones when you are away from them. Some may say, "I don't need to make a special covenant in order for God to see or watch over me or my family." This may be true in the sense that the "eyes of the LORD are on the righteous" and the "steps of a good man are ordered by the LORD" (Ps. 34:15; 37:23). However, although the Scriptures reveal the will and plan of God, the Almighty moves toward us and for us when we ask. We are told to ask in order to receive (Matt. 7:7).

There are several reasons we must ask. First, when asking, we are demonstrating that we believe what God has spoken. Second, there is a spiritual law that states that all the promises of God are released by asking and believing. Third, our faith is built and our joy is full when we ask and see God answer our prayers.

ESTABLISHING THE COVENANT

There are specific steps that we can take to establish the Mizpah covenant in our own lives:

1. Two must agree.

There is a unique authority when people come into perfect agreement. We are told, "If two of you agree on earth concerning anything that they ask, it will be done for them by My Father in heaven" (Matt. 18:19). The word *agree* is the Greek word *sumphoneo*, which means to be in harmony or in the same accord. We derive the English word *symphony* from this word. A symphony is the result of a combination of musical instruments that are all in tune and playing the same musical score.

The ability to agree and see results is more than mental assent or merely nodding *yes* to affirm something. The power of agreement must be an affirmation from deep within a person's spirit, from the very place deep within where the Holy Spirit dwells and where the Word of God can be felt. During the Mizpah covenant, both Laban and Jacob were in agreement. Laban asked God to watch his children, and Jacob agreed not to mistreat the women. It is possible that Laban was concerned that Jacob would mistreat Leah when she was no longer living at her father's home. After all, Jacob did not love Leah, as she was forced upon him. Rachel was the love of his life. Laban wanted Jacob to vow that he would treat his daughters well and not allow another woman to enter his life.

To enter a covenant of agreement that God will watch between the two of us when we are apart first involves the two individuals to come into full agreement.

2. Two must agree in prayer.

Prayer is more than a spiritual ritual. It is communication between the earth and heaven, humanity and God. As a child, I always wondered how long it took for God to hear my prayer. Growing up in church, I cannot recall ever hearing what happens to my words once they left my mouth. Did they go into the starry space and eventually float onward and upward until eventually reaching the ears of God?

I was in my teens before I noticed Revelation 5:8 (KJV):

> And when he had taken the book, the four beasts and four and twenty elders fell down before the Lamb, having every one of them harps, and golden vials full of odours, which are the prayers of saints.

The prayers of God's people (saints) are continually kept in golden vials before the throne of God. In the ancient temple, the priest would stand at the golden altar and mix hot coals of fire with sacred incense whose smoke would ascend upward into the special chamber called the holy place. The incense produced a special, sweet fragrance that filled the small chamber. One rabbi told me that all the prayers from God's people would come first to the ancient temple and gather over the golden altar. Each morning the incense was offered, the words would mix in with the prayers of the people and ascend to God in heaven. This was why Solomon taught that that if the Hebrew people were taken into captivity, they should pray facing toward Israel and Jerusalem (2 Chron. 6:37–38). Daniel practiced this in Babylonian captivity as he prayed with his windows opened facing Jerusalem (Dan. 6:10).

Our prayers are immediately before the throne of God and are stored in special vials. Thus, nothing we have prayed from a pure and sincere heart has ever fallen to the ground. When you agree in prayer and ask God to watch over one another, you must believe that the Lord has heard your words and will indeed perform what you have asked.

3. Two must confess.

Once we have prayed in full agreement according to the Word of God, we must then confess what we believe. The Bible says, "Let us hold fast the profession of our faith without wavering" (Heb. 10:23, KJV). Our confession is twofold. First is a confession to God: "I thank You, Lord, for Your covenant of protection, and I thank You for hearing me when I pray." We also confess one to another that we believe the Lord is going to watch over you and me when we are away from one another.

Confession is important because it continually places a seal upon what we have prayed and believed for. When we begin to speak out against our confession, we can actually hinder God's promises. When Zacharias doubted the word of Gabriel that his aged wife would have a son, he was stricken dumb for nine months (Luke 1:20). Israel was forbidden to inherit the Promised Land due to their constant complaining, which stemmed from their unbelief (Heb. 3:15–19).

I believe God enjoys providing protection for those in covenant with Him and in covenant with one another. One of the greatest God-ordained covenants is that of marriage. In the time of the early patriarchs, it was common for tribal leaders to have more than one wife and for them to take whatever women they chose without any opposition. Both Abraham and his son Isaac almost had their wives taken from them. God protected Sarah from Abimelech and also prevented Rebekah from falling into this Canaanite king's hands (Gen. 20, 26).

4. Two must pray with "all prayer."

When Paul wrote concerning the weapons of a believer's warfare in Ephesians 6, he compared our spiritual weaponry to the armor of a Roman soldier. He listed:

- Loin belt of truth (v. 14)
- Breastplate of righteousness (v. 14)
- Shoes of peace (v. 15)
- Shield of faith (v. 16)
- Helmet of salvation (v. 17)
- Sword of the Word of God (v. 17)

Having studied and completed a major teaching series on the armor of God, I noticed there appeared to be one significant, major weapon missing in Paul's analogy of the Roman armor to the Christian's armor, and that is the *lance*, or large spear, that each Roman soldier carried to battle. In my book on the armor of God, I wrote:

> The "pilums," or lances (also called javelins), were standard equipment when the Roman soldier was fully dressed in his armor. The Roman guard in Paul's prison cell may not have had his lances with him at the time Paul wrote the Book of Ephesians, because lances are weapons that are thrown for long distances, usually over twenty yards. This soldier was guarding Paul within the tight confines of a prison cell, and there was no need to be in full battle preparedness.
>
> When going into battle, the Roman soldier carried two lances. Both lances were approximately eighty inches long, but one was heavier than the other. The lighter lance weighed approximately four pounds, and

the heavier lance weighed about six pounds. The front part of the shaft was made of iron and had an arrow-like point at the end. The back half was made of ash wood. Lead weights were often added to the back end to balance the lance for longer-distance throwing and for greater impact when the lance hit its target.

The soldier would throw his lances while still a distance away from the enemy, before engaging in close combat, to hit either the enemy or his shield. If the lance hit the enemy, then that was one less enemy to fight. If the lance hit the enemy's shield, it would penetrate it deeply enough to make it very difficult to pull out and would therefore render the shield useless. The enemy would then have to leave his shield on the ground, thus making him more vulnerable to any attack. The iron section of the lance would bend upon impact, making it useless for the enemy to throw back at the Romans.[1]

While the lances are not listed by name in Ephesians 6, there is a passage that is important and is linked with the armor of God:

Praying always with all prayer and supplication in the Spirit, being watchful to this end with all perseverance and supplication for all the saints.

—EPHESIANS 6:18

I believe that Paul's reference to "all prayer" could be an allusion to the Roman soldier's lance, which is thrust through the atmosphere into the armor of the opponent. Prayer is not only communication to God, but it also brings salvation, healing, deliverance, and defeat to the powers of the enemy. Thus, prayer is both communication and a weapon of spiritual warfare.

"All prayer" means all kinds of prayer. Prayer, like a lance, is released from one location to impact a different location. Prayer can be classified into two basic categories: petition and praise. Both of these categories are spiritual weapons. So, we have petition and praise, just as the Roman soldier carried both a light lance and a heavier lance. What would the Christian soldier be without the weapons of prayer and praise?

As previously mentioned, the lance was balanced with weights. Likewise, the Christian's petitioning and worshiping must be balanced. You cannot have a church or a spiritual life that is all prayer or all praise. You must have both prayer and praise. We need to be balanced.

When we ask God to protect our loved one while we are apart, I believe the agreement is set when both people agree in prayer. However, just as incense was offered each morning at the temple, we must also come into agreement in our confession daily. I believe God can and will preserve and protect my family and me if we will follow His will without asking Him to do so over and over again. However, I still petition the Lord daily to bless and keep my family members from harm, danger, and disabling accidents. These prayers are my "lances" in my spiritual arsenal, which are shot into the atmosphere to stop the planned attacks of the enemy. A person should not wait until the problems arrive to suddenly say, "I think we should pray." We should be proactive and not just reactive. Just as it's better to eat right and exercise before heart trouble comes than to try to heal the damage after it happens, it's also better to be prepared for the enemy's attack before it comes.

These simple procedures will enable two or more people to enter into what I call *the Mizpah covenant*. God can and will protect those who carry our name and our DNA!

Chapter 10

THE COVENANT OVER
THE THRESHOLD

But when he was strong his heart was lifted up,
to his destruction, for he transgressed against
the LORD his God by entering the temple
of the LORD to burn incense on the altar of
incense.

—2 CHRONICLES 26:16

IN ANCIENT ISRAEL AND THROUGHOUT THE TRIBAL
culture of the Middle East and Africa, it was customary
to mark property and to set boundaries using stones. There
are natural and spiritual principles linked to setting forth a
line, both an invisible spiritual line and a visible set marker, to
prevent an outsider from *overstepping their bounds.*

In Scripture, markers could be large stone pillars (Gen.
28:18), piles of stones (Gen. 31:46), or even rivers, such as the
Jordan River, which served as the dividing line between Israel
and the land of Edom and Moab (Josh. 1:11–15).

When God revealed to Moses the instructions for the
construction of His holy tabernacle, He established three

distinct rooms—the outer court, the inner court, and the holy of holies—all separated by large handmade veils. The veils prevented common individuals from proceeding beyond certain points. Anyone attempting to break through the veils would not only experience death at the hands of the priest but would also encounter the immediate wrath and judgment of God (2 Chron. 26:16–21).

Marking the thresholds or the outer doorposts of the temple or the home created another type of boundary. Among the ancient Sumerians, Egyptians, and Babylonians, the temple of the god or goddess was the most sacred structure in the city. The large stone temples were the centers of spiritual activity and worship, and, in the earliest times, they also served as the places where the rich kept their money, concealed near the sacred inner chamber housing the shrine or idol. An Egyptian tour guide told me that it was believed that fear of the wrath of the gods would keep anyone from attempting to steal the wealth by passing the threshold into the place where the stone god was erected.

Several years ago in Israel we were touring the area of Bethshean, an early Roman city that was part of the famed Decapolis in Christ's day. While excavating near the city's main temple, the archeologist discovered the skeleton of a man who had gold coins in his clinched fist. A large marble column had fallen and killed him during an earthquake that destroyed the city in A.D. 749. The archeologist speculated that the fellow was in the temple when he felt the earthquake and grabbed an offering that was in the holy place of the temple.

THE GOD OF THE THRESHOLD

In early civilization, it was common for the heathen priests to erect large stone statues of the god and goddess at the entrances of the temple door to protect the temple. But eventually, people also began to mark the corners of their doors with special markings and objects in hopes that the gods would protect their homes. These were the gods of the thresholds.

For example, in ancient Sumer (the area of Iraq fifty-five hundred years ago), homes were often *marked* on the left and right upper posts with a carved image representing the god or goddess.

> THE ADVERSARY IS A COUNTERFEITER AND ATTEMPTS TO COPY THE TRUTH OF GOD, DISTORTING, TWISTING, AND DECEIVING MULTITUDES.

One of many examples was in the city of Uruk with a goddess called Inanna, associated with Venus and the moon, also known as the *queen of heaven*. Followers made ring posts out of reeds and carvings to put over the upper posts of the door, which were called *Inanna's knot*. The two markers for Inanna and other gods and goddesses used in similar ring posts held a cross pole, which stretched across the post from the left to the right. Thus, the corners of the outer post were *marked* by the god or goddess as a sign that a worshiper of that god or goddess lived in the home and in hopes that the god or goddess would protect those living inside.[1]

These protective false gods are found in every major ancient culture in and around the Middle East. The Babylonians had a winged creature called *Nergal*, which had a lion's body and a man's face with two wings connected to the body. It is interesting that the heavenly cherubim have the face of a lion and a man (Ezek. 41). The Babylonians believed that Nergal was also a solar deity and a god of war and pestilence, who also presided over the gates of the underworld.[2]

In Abraham's day the chief deity was named *Sin*. This idol deity was identified in stone carvings and bas-reliefs as a man with a beard of lapis who rode upon a winged bull. His symbol was a crescent moon, and his seat of power was believed to be in Ur in the south and Haran in the north. Abraham was from Ur (Gen. 11:28–31), and Abraham's father, Terah, was from Haran (Gen. 12:4–5).[3]

ALTARS NEAR THE THRESHOLDS

Christians are often unaware that altars were used in all early cultures to offer special offerings to their particular gods. Israeli archeologists point out that the Canaanites had numerous gods and would construct a four-horned altar made of stone to burn incense or to offer a burnt offering to their false deity. These altars were usually placed at the entrance of the temples where the people would watch the procedure. At times, the altars were located in front of the homes of the priests.

When considering all of this early information related to the importance of the threshold, or the outer doorposts of homes and temples, we should not be surprised that God instructed Israel to place the blood of the Passover lamb on the outer posts of the door. The two sides of the doors were called *posts*, and the upper section was the *lintel* (Exod. 12:22).

The ancient Egyptians understood this concept and knew the Hebrews were marking their houses for their God. The Egyptians, however, were unaware of the importance of this act in protecting firstborn Hebrew sons from the death angel during the famed Passover (Exod. 12). In ancient cultures, the firstborn son was dedicated to the god of the household. In the instance of the Hebrews, God required a special dedication offering when a son was born, and a redemption price was to be paid each time a nation's census counted the males over twenty years of age (Exod. 13:13; Num. 18:15).

When the tabernacle was constructed in the wilderness, God instructed Moses to place the brass altar of sacrifices in the outer court near the door (veiled entrance) of the tabernacle itself, which was located before the veil leading into the holy place. God also placed special handwoven curtains (veils) to set a physical boundary between the outer court and the other rooms designated strictly for the priests and the high priest.

We know that the adversary is a counterfeiter and attempts to copy the truth of God, distorting, twisting, and deceiving multitudes. The Almighty knew and understood the importance of the threshold and established spiritual laws and guidelines for His ancient chosen people, Israel, to follow.

RACHEL AND THE IMAGES

When Laban caught up with Jacob, he was angry that someone in Jacob's company had stolen his images of gods (in Hebrew, it is the word *teraphim*) from his house. The culprit was Laban's daughter Rachel, Jacob's favorite wife. Why would Rachel steal her father's idols? There are several opinions. The first suggestion is that there was a belief that these *gods* could inform the owner about the future; thus, Rachel believed (in ignorance) that her father's images could reveal where Jacob had gone. The Jewish historian Josephus stated that Rachel believed if she stole the images of her father's gods, and Laban threatened Jacob, she could use the images as leverage against him.[4] In ancient cultures, if a son-in-law possessed the household gods of his father-in-law, then he was considered a real son and shared in the inheritance.

These images, which in rabbinical literature can mean "disgraceful things," are used in the Bible to refer to idols. When the children of Israel took possession of the Promised Land, these images were often consulted for answers about the future. Consulting the images was one of the major sins God often charged Israel with and rebuked them because the idols could not predict the future. (See Isaiah 44–45.)

Jacob's real inheritance was not in Syria with Laban but in the Promised Land where his father, Isaac, and grandfather Abraham had confirmed a land covenant with God. Thus, these idols were as useless as the stone from which they were carved.

MARKING THE THRESHOLD

When the Hebrew fathers slew a lamb on the evening of the Passover, the blood of the lamb marked the two side posts and the upper lintel of their doors. This is a clear image of what was to come in the future crucifixion of the Messiah. These three blood marks represented the three crosses on Golgotha—one man on either side (the left and right) and Christ hanging on the cross in the middle (Matt. 27:38).

The Hebrew word for *posts*, found in Exodus 12, is the word *mezuzah*. In my book *Breaking the Jewish Code*, I have a chapter that deals with the Jewish concept of marking the post of the doors with an object called a *mezuzah*.

An actual kosher mezuzah has the words of the *Shema* (Deut. 6:4–9) and a passage from Deuteronomy 11:13–21 written by a trained scribe on a small parchment made from the skin of a kosher animal (cow or sheep). The name of God is written on the backside of the parchment, and the tiny scroll is rolled up and placed in the mezuzah case.

The case is usually a decorated case made of ceramic, stone, copper, silver, glass, wood, or even pewter. The designs vary and are not spiritually significant, but the parchment itself holds the significance of the mezuzah. Most mezuzahs have the Hebrew letter *shin*, the twenty-first letter of the Hebrew alphabet, on the outer surface, which represents the first letter in God's name, *Shaddai*. The name *Shaddai* is a name that serves as an acronym for "guardian of the doorways of Israel." The box is designed to protect the parchment from the weather or other elements that could harm the ink.

Some scholars have suggested that the purpose for the mezuzah was to remind the Jewish people, on a continual basis, of the blood of the lamb, which, when applied on the door-post in Egypt, prevented the destroying angel from entering the home and killing the firstborn. This theory, however, is an opinion and is not based on the rabbinical understanding of the purpose of the mezuzah.

Some Jews, identified as mystics, tend to see the mezuzah as some form of a charm designed to ward off evil spirits, but this is certainly not the original intent. It is intended to be a reminder to those living in the home that the house has been dedicated to God; thus, those living therein should commit to walk in accordance with God's Word. It is viewed, however, as an object reminding God to protect the home. The Talmud teaches that a proper mezuzah *can* bring long life and protection to the household. A Talmudic story tells of a king who gave a diamond to a rabbi as a present. In return, the rabbi gave the king a mezuzah, which insulted the king. The rabbi commented to the king, "I will have to hire guards to protect my home because of the gift you gave me, but the gift I gave will protect your home."

THE PROTECTION OF OUR DOORS

Religious Jews mark their homes with the mezuzah. How should believers mark their homes with a protective covenant? Just as the blood of an earthly lamb served as a restraint against the death angel of Egypt, the precious blood of Christ not only serves as the foundation of our redemption but also is the strongest spiritual weapon against our spiritual adversary. We read in Revelation 12:

> And they overcame him [Satan] by the blood of the Lamb and by the word of their testimony, and they did not love their lives to the death.
>
> —REVELATION 12:11

Christ shed His blood more than nineteen hundred years ago, and today humanity can receive redemption by asking God to forgive their sins and cleanse them by the blood of the final *Lamb*, Jesus Christ (John 1:29; 1 John 1:9). How can we *apply* the protective blood of Christ over our homes in much the same manner the blood of the Passover lamb kept the destroyer out?

Our protection is formed in the same manner as our redemption is received—through faith and confession. If you "confess with your mouth the Lord Jesus and believe in your heart that God has raised Him from the dead, you will be saved" (Rom. 10:9). The blood of Christ is applied to our hearts when we believe, ask, and then confess. The Greek word for *confess* means "to speak the same thing, to agree with, and to admit." When we pray, we are petitioning God, but when we confess, we are agreeing with God. When we are converted, we do not literally see blood dripping from the heavenly temple, entering our physical hearts or spirits. However, we can feel the burden of sin lift and sense a relief from the burden of guilt.

If we are to confess the power of the blood of Christ over our home, we should pray:

> *Heavenly Father, in Christ's sacred and holy name, I approach Your heavenly temple and ask You to protect my home, my companion, and my children through the power of the blood of Christ. Father, I acknowledge that Your people were protected from the destroyer during Passover by the lamb's blood, and I confess the power of Christ's blood to redeem us from destruction and provide protection for my household and me.*

I recall teaching my children to pray a prayer of protection over our home. When my son was only five years of age, he would pray, "God, protect our house, and don't let anything happen to it." On one occasion, the family was outside the mainland when two men with ski masks attempted to break into our home. Before they could, they were exposed, and the police came and arrested them. I told my son, "Your prayers were heard, and the

Lord defended our house from these intruders."

I have taught my children and the partners of our ministry that the Old Testament symbolisms, customs, and rituals are pictures of things that were to come (Col. 2:16–17). Under the old covenant, Moses was instructed to offer a lamb in the morning and one in the evening. The morning is when we begin our day, and the evening is when we pray to end the day and to rest for the evening. I believe the spiritual principle is that we must begin and conclude our day with the Lord. We must also confess His cleansing and protective blood in both the morning and the evening.

The power of the blood sacrifices is seen throughout the Old Testament. We have spoken of the Exodus, but on another occasion, an angel with a sword stood over the Mount of Olives, ready to target Jerusalem with a plague. David immediately ran to the top of Mount Moriah, where Abraham had offered Isaac hundreds of years before (Gen. 22:1–2), and David purchased the threshing floor of Ornan the Jebusite, built an altar, and offered a blood offering, after which the angel put away his sword. (See 1 Chronicles 21:19–30.)

Certainly, if Christ's blood can cleanse the vilest sinners and change their bodies to temples of the Holy Spirit where the living God dwells (1 Cor. 3:15–16), then certainly when we confess the power of Christ's blood, we have not only the attention of God but also the attention of the angels of the covenant! Angels are attracted to God's Word:

> Bless the LORD, you His angels,
> Who excel in strength, who do His word,
> Heeding the voice of His word.
>
> —PSALM 103:20

Chapter 11

FASTING—GAINING THE ATTENTION OF THE HEAVENLY MESSENGERS

But after long abstinence from food, then Paul stood in the midst of them and said, "...For there stood by me this night an angel of the God to whom I belong...saying, 'Do not be afraid.'"

—ACTS 27:21–24

IN 1950, THE KOREAN WAR SUDDENLY ERUPTED. DALE Smith and C. M. Morgan, two young men from the small towns of Atwell and Raysal, West Virginia, had been drafted into the army and had been serving in Korea. During a huge offensive, the North Koreans drove the American forces back, and both young men were missing in action. Dale's mother, who attended the Atwell Church of God, was contacted by the army and told that her son was missing and assumed dead.

After hearing this news, Dale's mother, a precious saint of God, stood during a church service and requested prayer for her son. She confessed that she did not believe her son was dead, and she wanted God's divine intervention to bring him home. The church began to intercede fervently.

My father, Fred Stone, eighteen years old at the time, experienced a dream in which he saw an area surrounded by barbed-wire fences and covered with shaggy huts and terrible living conditions. Dad saw both of the young men who were missing in action and assumed dead. In the dream, Dale's hands were on the barbed wire, and he said, "Fred, tell my mother that I am not dead, but I am in a North Korean prison camp. Tell her that if she will pray, I will live and get out." In the dream, Dad said, "I will tell her."

A few days later, Dad had someone drive him to the church, and he personally spoke to Mrs. Smith and related the entire dream to her. The mother began to rejoice and believed the dream was from the Lord. The mother and certain church members fasted and prayed for several weeks, agreeing that her son was alive and would return home. In the meantime, the military contacted the mother and offered her insurance money on behalf of her son, whom they believed was slain in the battle. She refused, saying she believed he was alive and that God would bring him home!

Several months later, Dad was traveling on a bus that pulled into a small bus station in War, West Virginia. Dad was amazed to read the headlines of the town's newspaper, which read: "Two Local Men Released in Pyongyang Prison Exchange." Dad picked up the paper, and there were the high school photos of Dale Smith and C. M. Morgan! Both men were released and returned to West Virginia. The Lord protected them because of the *prayer and fasting* of righteous people.

THE SUPERNATURAL POWER OF FASTING

Fasting was an important practice in both Old and New Testaments and is mentioned in Scripture more than forty times. Prayer combined with fasting is a powerful weapon in the believer's arsenal. In Matthew 17:15–21, Jesus taught that certain types of evil spirits can only be expelled through prayer and fasting, as fasting can diminish the presence of unbelief in a person's life. There are various opinions as to what actually constitutes a true fast, but by definition *a fast* is a set period of time in which a person voluntarily abstains from food. The strict definition of the term means to "shut the mouth," to avoid eating. It is described as "humbling" or "chastening" the soul (Ps. 35:13; 69:10).

When a person initiates a fast, the first few days are often difficult to get through, as headaches (sometimes caffeine withdrawals), hunger pains, and physical tiredness can occur. I have learned from experience that often after the third day, the headaches, hunger pains, and other discomforts cease, and a person often begins to feel spiritually, emotionally, and even physically clearer and better than prior to the fast.

Both devout Christians and Jews practice fasting at different seasons. Among the Jewish people there are yearly fast days: These include:

- The fast of the firstborn, commemorating the salvation of the firstborn sons in Egypt

- The seventh of Tammuz, the day commemorating the breaking down of the wall of Jerusalem

- The ninth of Av, remembering the tragedies of the Jewish people

- Yom Kippur, the fast on the Day of Atonement every year on the tenth of Tishri

- The tenth of Tevat, a fast commemorating the fall of Jerusalem

- The fast of Esther on the thirteenth of Adar, the day before Purim

When commemorating events through a fast, such as the Jews do, a person must be cautious not to lose the original meaning or purpose of the fast. Fasting must be for a pure and righteous motive. Christ rebuked the Pharisees for fasting to be seen of men and in order to appear to be more spiritual than others. These self-righteous hypocrites would disfigure their faces and put on a sad countenance so people would view them as men of great humility who were afflicting their souls to be closer to God (Matt. 6:16–18).

Two men who were my mentors in ministry, my father and Dr. T. L. Lowery, both consistently practiced fasting throughout their ministry. Following his fasts, Dad always received a special word from the Lord or the spiritual under-standing he needed at the time. Dr. Lowery has fasted for forty days, drinking only water. He has received supernatural visitations from the Lord and direct instructions for his life and ministry during and following lengthy fasts. On several occasions, God sent heavenly messengers to both of these men through dreams or visions, giving them needed instructions and words of wisdom for the season they were in.

FASTING CAN BRING ANGELIC ASSISTANCE

In Acts 27, the apostle Paul was a prisoner on a ship with 276 passengers on board. Launching the voyage in the winter, the ship headed into a violent sea storm, called Euroclydon. The ship tossed like a leaf in the wind and was in danger of splitting into pieces. No stars or light from the moon was seen for many days, and because of the dangerous rocks and quicksand, it appeared that Paul and the passengers would drown in the murky waters. Paul had been on an *extended fast* and was *praying* for God's intervention. God released a heavenly messenger to bring Paul this encouraging word:

> But after long abstinence from food, then Paul stood in the midst of them and said, "Men, you should have listened to me, and not have sailed from Crete and incurred this disaster and loss. And now I urge you to take heart, for there will be no loss of life among you, but only of the ship. For there stood by me this night an angel of the God to whom I belong and whom I serve, saying, 'Do not be afraid, Paul; you must be brought before Caesar; and indeed God has granted you all those who sail with you.'"
>
> —ACTS 27:21–24

In the midst of a life-threatening storm, God sent assurance through an angelic messenger that the ship would be destroyed, but not one of the 276 passengers, many of whom were prisoners, would die in the process.

After Christ was baptized by John in the Jordan River, He was then directed by the Holy Spirit to spend days in solitude, fasting and praying (Matt. 4). After forty days, the tempter

(Satan) came and began to harass Christ, demanding He prove He was the Son of God. The temptation involved three aspects:

- *Lust of the flesh*—turn the stones into bread to eat

- *Lust of the eyes*—throw Yourself from the high point of the temple so angels can rescue You

- *Pride of life*—bow and worship Satan, and he will give You the world's kingdoms

Following the fast and the testing from Satan, Christ was physically weak, and the heavenly Father sent angels to personally minister to Him:

> Then the devil left Him, and behold, angels came and ministered to Him.
>
> —MATTHEW 4:11

Toward the conclusion of Christ's ministry, when He was in agony in the Garden of Gethsemane, we read that, "Then an angel appeared to Him from heaven, strengthening Him" (Luke 22:43). Thus, during the two most stressful moments in Christ's life—His forty-day fast and prior to His crucifixion—angels were commissioned to personally minister to Him and strengthen Him. This would have included not only physical strength but emotional and spiritual strength as well.

During my earlier ministry, I lived what I call a "fasting life." Instead of eating throughout the week and selecting a specific day to fast, I would often go days on end without eating, or eat only one time a day just to maintain strength. When fasting, my spiritual *senses* were sharper and keener, and I was able to discern both good and evil more clearly. I could also sense when there was a strategy of the enemy or some form of danger that lay ahead.

Early one morning, I departed from Northport, Alabama, and was traveling by car on a four-hour drive to Mississippi. I recall being very tired, and several times I found my eyes becoming heavy. I would play music and roll down the window to help me stay awake. Without realizing it, I dozed off. Suddenly I was struck in the back of my shoulders by what felt like a man's hand. The sudden *slap* did not hurt, but it jerked me forward, awaking me. Unknowingly, I had already veered off the road and was driving head-on toward the corner of an interstate bridge. I had a split second to jerk the car away from the bridge and barely miss colliding head-on with the concrete support. I began to cry because there was no one else in the car, and I knew the Lord had sent a heavenly messenger on my behalf to protect me.

Fasting is like a magnet that attracts your soul and spirit closer to the heavenly realm. Isaiah wrote about the power of fasting and revealed that a fast would: "loose the bonds of wickedness…undo the heavy burdens…let the oppressed go free, and…break every yoke" (Isa. 58:6). In verse 8 (KJV) Isaiah predicted:

> Then shall thy light break forth as the morning, and thine health shall spring forth speedily: and thy righteousness shall go before thee; the glory of the LORD shall be *thy rereward*.

> —EMPHASIS ADDED

Notice that God will be thy "rereward." Believers often read this as "thy reward," but it is not *reward* but the word *rereward*.

In each of the other five biblical verses where the word *rereward* is used, it alludes to someone bringing up the back part of the camp or of being in the flank or the rear guard of an army. It has this same meaning in this Isaiah passage. When we fast and earnestly seek God, He has us covered from the back side. He can prevent the adversary from a "sneak attack" that would catch you off guard!

In ancient Israel, the Syrian army would prepare secret battle plans against Israel, and God would reveal their strategy to Elisha, thereby warning Israel and preventing the success of the attacks. The Syrian leader discovered Elisha's prayer life and sent an army to capture the prophet. One morning the prophet and his servant stood on a hilltop and saw a huge advancing army surrounding the mountain. Scripture reveals that Elisha was surrounded by "horses and chariots of fire" (2 Kings 6:17). This is an example of God becoming our rear guard and protecting our back.

> FASTING IS LIKE A MAGNET THAT ATTRACTS YOUR SOUL AND SPIRIT CLOSER TO THE HEAVENLY REALM.

Thus, not only does fasting diminish unbelief, renew our faith, and increase the level of God's presence to break yokes and bondages, but it also helps form a protective hedge that will surround us.

ANGELS AND FAMILY SALVATION

I believe that angels can also be involved in family salvation. Angels cannot provide salvation; only Christ can. However, angels can help connect a believer and an unbeliever, thus giving the unsaved person an opportunity to hear and receive a clear message of the gospel.

Such was the case in Acts 10. Cornelius was of Italian descent and a centurion in the Roman army. He is identified as "a devout man and one who feared God with all his household, who gave alms generously to the people, and prayed to God always" (Acts 10:2). During his prayer time at the ninth hour of the day, he received a vision of an angel telling him, "Your prayers and your alms have come up for a memorial before God" (v. 4). What exactly does this statement mean?

We must explore the heavenly temple revealed in the Book of Revelation to understand this statement. There are so many angels in the heavenly city that they are called "an innumerable company" (Heb. 12:22). However, certain angels are given specific assignments. There is an angel over fire (Rev. 14:18) and an angel given a key to the abyss (Rev. 9:1). We read of an angel offering incense before the golden altar in heaven (Rev. 8:3–5). The golden altar in the earthly temple was the place where the priest would burn incense each morning, representing the prayers of the Hebrew people ascending up to God. The psalmist wrote, "Let my prayer be set before You as incense" (Ps. 141:2).

At least eleven different types of prayer are recorded in the New Testament, including:

1. Prayer of confession of sins—1 John 1:9

2. Prayer of confessing our faults—James 5:16

3. Prayer of agreement—Matthew 18:19

4. Prayer of faith for the sick—James 5:15

5. Prayer of binding—Matthew 16:19

6. Prayer of loosing—Matthew 16:19

7. Praying in the Spirit—Ephesians 6:18

8. Praying in the Spirit with understanding—
1 Corinthians 14:15

9. Prayer of thanksgiving—Philippians 4:6

10. Prayer of intercession—1 Timothy 2:1

11. Prayer for general supplication—Philippians 4:6

When we pray, our words are stored in golden vials in heaven:

> And when he had taken the book, the four beasts and four and twenty elders fell down before the Lamb, having every one of them harps, and golden vials full of odours, which are the prayers of saints.
>
> —Revelation 5:8, kjv

This should encourage us that the words of our prayers do not float throughout the galaxy, allowing God to randomly pull one from the starry space as the "lucky one" to get a prayer answered. Our words are stored in special vials in the heavenly temple, before the very throne of the eternal Creator!

In the case of Cornelius, this faithful servant of the Lord had mixed his prayers with his giving, and his words and actions "have come up for a memorial before God" (Acts 10:4). What is this memorial? The word here means "to keep alive the memory of something or someone." It is a reminder set to remember something.

The prophet Malachi wrote of a special book in heaven that

contained the names of righteous individuals, called a *book of remembrance.*

> Then those who feared the LORD spoke to one another,
> And the LORD listened and heard them;
> So a book of remembrance was written before Him
> For those who fear the LORD
> And who meditate on His name.
>
> —MALACHI 3:16

We know there are numerous books in heaven that contain names, such as the Lamb's Book of Life (Rev. 3:5). This special book of remembrance is for those who fear the Lord and is linked to giving of finances. (See Malachi 3.) The memorial in heaven mentioned in the story of Cornelius may have been this book of remembrance with the name of Cornelius recorded in it! God was observing Cornelius as he prayed and gave, and He was *marking him* and his entire family for a special spiritual blessing.

The angel appeared in this vision and connected this Italian man with the apostle Peter. It was Peter, a Jew, who entered the home of this Gentile family and explained the gospel, which resulted in Cornelius seeing his family receive the fullness of the Spirit (Acts 10:34–47). As a Jew, at the time Peter was quite prejudiced against Gentiles. Yet God gave Peter a vision to prepare him for his encounter with this Gentile family (Acts 10:11–20). God had marked the Gentile's home for a blessing, and the special angel linked the right man at the right time.

Many believers have family members who are outside of the covenant of faith and have no relationship with Christ. Believers are concerned about the eternal destiny of such persons. Often they will attempt to reach out to the unconverted person with love, compassion, and spiritual information, only to be shunned and rejected because of unbelief.

Our first concern is their protection. Each day individuals die from drug overdoses, alcohol abuse, tragic accidents, and heart failure. One man shared with me that his son, in his twenties, was on drugs and continuing a dangerous lifestyle. He said, "I have always heard that eventually his ability to make good judgments would develop in his brain—I hope it does because I am praying now that he will stay alive long enough to turn from his destructive ways."

When an individual is in covenant with God, that person can intercede on behalf of family members because they carry your name and your bloodline. God was willing to spare Lot because he and Abraham were blood kin, and whoever carried the blood of Abraham could receive special favor from the Lord as intercession was made. When Paul was speaking of ministering spirits (angels) he said:

> Are they not all ministering spirits sent forth to minister for those who will inherit salvation?
>
> —HEBREW 1:14

Two other translations read:

> Are not all angels ministering spirits sent to serve those who will inherit salvation?
>
> —NIV

> Are not the angels all ministering spirits (servants) sent out in the service [of God for the assistance] of those who are to inherit salvation?
>
> —AMP

When reading these three translations, one could suggest that this passage alludes not just to angels ministering to believers but to angels that are assigned in God's service to minister to those who shall (future tense) inherit salvation. If you have an unconverted family member, then ask the Lord to send a heavenly messenger to protect that person from a premature death and connect him or her with a believer who can present a clear gospel message to your family member. Many individuals are won to Christ through the witness of a close friend or work colleague.

Years ago a mother was burdened for her son who was linking with the wrong crowd. Raised in church, he was departing from his early training and moving into the dangerous world of drugs and alcohol. I was inspired to tell her to pray for God to send a "kingdom connection" to her son, perhaps a girlfriend or a male friend who was a strong believer and could direct him back to the truth. I suggested she ask God to send an angel of the Lord to arrange this connection. Months later she came to me rejoicing and telling me that her son had met a strong Christian girl, and he was now attending church with her and had separated from the bad influences!

We must never underestimate the power and influence of these ministering spirits who can be commissioned to link people together and provide protection for our family.

THEN WHY DOES TRAGEDY OCCUR?

If God protects people, then why do tragedies occur? In the early 1990s I was a guest on a worldwide weekly Christian program. The guest prior to my live interview had given a heart-wrenching story of how his loving son had been killed in an accident involving parachuting from a plane. I confess I felt uncomfortable as I, the next guest, began to share about God's protective power and the ministry of angels. I caught a glimpse of the parents out of the corner of my eye, and instead of giving looks of frustration or anger, they were nodding their heads. It was then I realized a great truth. Just because we have a negative experience in life does not diminish the promises in Scripture. However, this sort of *contradiction* develops as a person may ask, "If God heals, why did my child die?" or "If God can protect us, why did this Christian die in a car accident?"

This type of question is common, especially when a tragedy or premature death strikes a family. Yet, when we read the Scriptures, there are several incidents in the lives of the prophets and apostles that reveal a strange paradox. The first involves the prophet Elisha. Prior to Elijah's supernatural departure to heaven, this great man of God was already personally ministering to Elijah. It was Elisha who followed Elijah across the Jordan River and requested a "double portion of Elijah's anointing" to be transferred to him (2 Kings 2). This special prayer was answered, and Elisha not only received a double portion, but he also performed twice as many miracles as Elijah! In fact, Elisha was so filled with the Spirit of God that long after his death a dead man was thrown into the grave of Elisha, and the healing power still in the bones of Elisha raised the man from the dead (2 Kings 13:21).

With all of this "power" resting on Elisha, we would assume that he should be exempt from sickness and live a long, long life. However, we read how he died:

> Elisha had become sick with the illness of which he
> would die.
>
> —2 KINGS 13:14

How could a prophet with so much anointing power that his dried bones could raise a man from the dead have a sickness? Wouldn't the anointing of the Holy Spirit drive out the disease? In explaining this, we must remember that we are *body, soul, and spirit* (1 Thess. 5:23). The body will age, and we are only promised a certain number of years in life (Ps. 90:10). Once we reach our full number of days, we will die, as the Scripture says: "It is appointed for men to die once, but after this the judgment" (Heb. 9:27). Our departure will be by one or a combination of things—natural causes such as our hearts simply quitting, by some form of infirmity, or by some accident.

There is a misconception among some that the precious anointing of the Holy Spirit will somehow exempt a believer from personal attacks or from any form of sickness or disease. David was anointed on three separate occasions: first as a teenager, second to be the king of Judah, and finally as the king of Israel. David had the precious anointing oil poured over him by the prophet Samuel, yet after years of confrontation with Saul, David wrote, "And I am weak today, though anointed king" (2 Sam. 3:39).

The anointing of the Holy Spirit often attracts the attention of the kingdom of darkness. When Christ was baptized in water, the Holy Spirit came upon him. Immediately He was led into the wilderness where He engaged Satan in a forty-day conflict (Matt 4:1–2). Just as David was anointed and the many battles had brought a weakness to his mind and body, Christ was anointed, yet the anointing did not prevent temptation from coming against His mind. Elisha was anointed, yet Elisha also died sick. It is a strange paradox.

A second example is found in the Book of Acts. King Herod had arrested James and later had him beheaded. Peter was arrested and placed in prison, and his beheading was planned for after Passover (Acts 12). The church heard of Peter's predicament and of the danger to his life, and they engaged in nonstop all-night prayer meetings. Because of their intercession, an angel of the Lord was commissioned to the prison where Peter was chained and released him from the jail. Peter actually thought he was dreaming or having a vision until he found himself outside the prison walls (Acts 12:5–11).

Now here is the paradox. Why did God allow James to be beheaded and not Peter? I have suggested two reasons. First, Jesus had already predicted that Peter would live to be an old man, and at the time of his arrest he was still a young minister (John 21:18). Thus, Peter could sleep well knowing that his appointed time had not yet come. Second, once the church heard of James's death and Peter's arrest, they "prayed without ceasing " for Peter's release (Acts 12:5, KJV). These prayers were heard, and the angelic messenger supernaturally delivered Peter from his death sentence. James and Peter were both leaders in the church, and yet one was slain and the other was spared.

The same occurs today. Good people who have a relationship with Christ are taken to heaven through accidents, diseases, and other tragedies.

We must remember that the many promises in the Word of God are not activated in your personal life just because they are recorded in the Holy Bible. For example, we read that God loved this world so much that He gave His only begotten

Son to die for us (John 3:16). However, a person is not automatically saved just because that verse is in the Bible. A person must believe with his or her heart and confess with the mouth the Lord Jesus Christ, and "they shall be saved" (Rom. 10:13). Salvation has been provided, but it can only be imparted by faith and confession.

Healing is a provision in both covenants. God told the Hebrew nation: "I am the LORD who heals you" (Exod. 15:26). In the New Testament, Peter wrote of Christ sufferings and declared: "By whose stripes you were healed" (1 Pet. 2:24). At the time of Israel's departure from Egypt, the Hebrew people were instructed to eat a lamb and strike the outer posts of their doorframes with the blood of the lamb. We later read that the angel of death bypassed the homes of the Hebrews, sparing the firstborn sons, and the entire nation came out of Egypt with not a sick or feeble person among them. This was a picture of the perfect sacrifice, Jesus Christ, whose blood brought redemption and whose body (stripes) would bring healing (Isa. 53).

These promises of healing do not impact a person just because God spoke them or a prophet wrote them. An individual must read or hear and believe the Word of God and then ask God to fulfill His Word in his or her life.

God has provided us access to His angels through our fasting and prayer. As you continue reading in the following chapter, you will discover that God has also made possible *long-distance intercession* by providing His Son Christ as our "heavenly mediator"!

Chapter 12

THE MIRACLE OF LONG-DISTANCE INTERCESSION

Are they not all ministering spirits sent forth to
minister for those who will inherit salvation?

—HEBREWS 1:14

WHEN I WAS A CHILD, I WOULD LIE IN BED NEAR A
window and look into the dark sky at the thousands
of stars twinkling like lights on a Christmas tree and think
to myself, "God is so far up there; how can He hear me when
I pray?" I am certain many people, not just children, have
thought this.

Throughout the New Testament, various passages allude to
"intercession" being made on behalf of another person. Christ
is our heavenly High Priest who stands before the heavenly
Father and makes "intercession for [us]" (Heb. 7:25). As our
heavenly mediator, He represents us before God just as a
lawyer would in a courtroom. As Satan, the accuser of the
brethren, stands before the heavenly court to hurl accusations
against the believer, Christ is present to resist those slanderous

accusations and present us as innocent through His redeeming and cleansing blood (Rev. 1:5).

> ONE OF THE GREAT DUTIES OF THE HOLY SPIRIT IS TO BE OUR ADVOCATE ON EARTH AND TO PRAY THROUGH US, EVEN WHEN WE ARE UNCERTAIN OF WHAT TO PRAY FOR.

The Greek words for "intercede" or "intercession" in the New Testament are interesting. They can have the meaning of meeting with a person to form a conversation and make a petition. According to W. E. Vine, one of the words, *enteuxis*, is used in ancient papyri for a technical term of approaching a king (as on behalf of another).[1]

The various Greek words translated as "intercession" or "intercessions" all allude to a person standing before God on behalf of another and petitioning the Lord on that person's behalf.

> Likewise the Spirit also helps in our weaknesses. For we do not know what we should pray for as we ought, but the Spirit Himself makes intercession for us with groanings which cannot be uttered. Now He who searches the hearts knows what the mind of the Spirit is, because He makes intercession for the saints according to the will of God.
>
> —ROMANS 8:26–27

The Holy Spirit is called the "Comforter" (John 14:16, KJV). When we think of a comforter, we imagine a person rubbing our shoulders and saying, "Don't worry; it's OK." The word

Comforter in John 14:16 is *parakletos*, which means one who goes alongside of to help. Again, *Vine's* comments:

> It was used in a court of justice to denote a legal assistant, counsel for the defense, and advocate; then generally, one who pleads another's cause, an intercessor, advocate as in 1 John 2:1 of the Lord Jesus.[2]

ANCIENT INTERCESSION USED BY ABRAHAM AND MOSES

The power of intercessory prayer is not a new revelation in the New Testament. It was a powerful spiritual tool used in the first covenant in the times of Abraham and Moses. Both men understood the relationship of their covenant with God as "covenant men" and the spiritual authority they carried as they approached the heavenly throne room and requested special favors of God.

Example of Abraham

Abraham's nephew, Lot, had moved his family into the city of Sodom (Gen. 13:12). The iniquity of the city reached heaven, and God targeted the city for destruction. Abraham was marked as God's covenant representative on Earth, and the Almighty would not hide the plan of destruction from Abraham, since his blood kin was living in the city. In Genesis 18, Abraham begins a negotiation with God concerning the city of Sodom. He requests that if God can find fifty righteous people, He will spare the city. The Lord agrees to stop the destruction for fifty. Abraham lowers the expectations from fifty to forty, then to thirty...twenty...and finally stops at ten. If God found ten righteous people, would He spare the city? The Lord agreed to spare Sodom for ten righteous people. (See Genesis 18.)

The destruction proceeded because God could not find ten; He found only four—Lot, his wife, and his two daughters (Gen. 19:16). Why did Abraham stop with the number ten and not four? Because Lot had daughters and sons-in-law who did not leave the city because they did not believe destruction was coming:

> So Lot went out and spoke to his sons-in-law, who had married his daughters, and said, "Get up, get out of this place; for the LORD will destroy this city!" But to his sons-in-law he seemed to be joking.
>
> —GENESIS 19:14

When the sun was risen upon the earth, God's fiery judgment destroyed the cities of the plain. Although warned against doing so, Lot's wife looked back and was killed as a result. I believe she was looking back because she knew she was losing daughters and sons-in-law in the destruction of the city (Gen. 19:26). Abraham's intercession prevented the death of Lot and his daughters. It took a man who understood his covenant relationship with God to stand in the gap for his family and prevent their premature deaths!

After Abraham interceded for Lot in chapter 18, we read in chapter 19 where God commissioned two angels in the form of men to go to the city to warn Lot and to lead him out of the city prior to when the wrath of God would strike the wicked place (Gen. 19:1). This one verse indicates that angels can appear in the form of a man and bring protection of a message from God. Paul alluded to this in Hebrews when he said:

> Do not forget to entertain strangers, for by so doing some have unwittingly entertained angels.
>
> —Hebrews 13:2

Example of Moses

The second great example of intercession happens when Moses received the Law on the mountain and then, after forty days, returned to the camp of Israel to find that the people were worshiping an idol of a golden cow. God, in His anger, was determined to destroy Israel and raise up a new nation through Moses:

> And the LORD said to Moses, "Go, get down! For your people whom you brought out of the land of Egypt have corrupted themselves. They have turned aside quickly out of the way which I commanded them. They have made themselves a molded calf, and worshiped it and sacrificed to it, and said, 'This is your god, O Israel, that brought you out of the land of Egypt!'" And the LORD said to Moses, "I have seen this people, and indeed it is a stiff-necked people! Now therefore, let Me alone, that My wrath may burn hot against them and I may consume them. And I will make of you a great nation." Then Moses pleaded with the LORD his God, and said: "LORD, why does Your wrath burn hot against Your people whom You have brought out of the land of Egypt with great power and with a mighty hand? Why should the Egyptians speak, and say, 'He brought them out to harm them, to kill them in the mountains,

and to consume them from the face of the earth'? Turn from Your fierce wrath, and relent from this harm to Your people. Remember Abraham, Isaac, and Israel, Your servants, to whom You swore by Your own self, and said to them, 'I will multiply your descendants as the stars of heaven; and all this land that I have spoken of I give to your descendants, and they shall inherit it forever.'" So the LORD relented from the harm which He said He would do to His people.

—EXODUS 32:7–14

Moses understood that the Almighty had sworn an oath to Abraham that his descendants would become a great nation. From Abraham's promise to the Exodus is four hundred thirty years (Exod. 12:40). During this time, the nation of Israel grew from one man, Abraham, to more than six hundred thousand men of war (Exod. 12:37). Because of their idolatry, God was willing to destroy these six hundred thousand men along with their children and wives. Moses knew God was true to His covenant and reminded God of His eternal agreement with Abraham. God "relented," or changed His mind, and reversed His decision concerning the Hebrew nation.

This is a dynamic example of a human interceding on behalf of another. In many instances, intercession is linked to preventing danger or even premature death coming upon a person. There have been several times in my life when intercession spared my own life.

HANGING ON A VOLCANIC RIM

In the late 1980s, I traveled to Crater Lake State Park in Oregon with a close friend, Keith Dudley. There is an island in middle of Crater Lake called Wizard Island. A boat brought us to a small dock, where we began a long, zigzagging hike up a trail to the top of this small volcanic island. Time was nearing for the last boat to pick up the folks on the island, and I had a bright idea—instead of walking the normal trail down, I would travel down the backside of the volcano and explore the area. It was very steep and high up, and I was walking sideways with a fifteen-pound backpack.

I came to an area where lava had flowed centuries earlier from the top to the bottom of the extinct volcano. I did not realize how slippery it was. I fell and began rolling. I knew there was jagged, sharp volcanic rock at the bottom, and if I continued to roll, I would land on the rock, breaking bones and possibly killing myself. I screamed out, "God, help me!" Suddenly, I stopped, lying facedown on my stomach. I lay there, knowing if I moved I would continue to slide downward. Every time I attempted to move, I slid and frantically attempted to dig my fingers into the ground. There were only slippery rocks and dirt and really nothing to hold on to—no shrubs, trees, or branches. Total fear gripped me, and for the first time I understood what it was to feel a "spirit of death." I was in anguish, not knowing how to make it across the wide, barren place to the large trees growing on the other side. As I prayed and begged the Lord for His help, I noticed a small piece of wood about eight inches long near my right hand. The thought came to take this small stick and jab it into the ground to help hold me up. I grabbed it with my right hand suddenly but began sliding again. As I thrust the stick into the ground, it held my body weight. Using this method, I was able to eventually make it to the other side, clearing the wide, dangerous area that was barren.

When I finally arrived at the boat dock, Keith said, "Man, what happened? I was getting worried about you!"

I said, "The Lord literally delivered me from death!" When I returned home, my father called and began to question me: "Perry, where were you on Thursday at about six o'clock?" I asked him why, and he replied, "I was driving with your mother through Knoxville, Tennessee, and I felt such a heavy burden that your life was in great danger. I began to pray in the Holy Spirit for about an hour before I gained any relief."

I told him it was Thursday when I was sliding down the slick side of a volcanic island, and my life was literally *hanging in the balance*. But the time was different; he said it was six o'clock, and according to my watch, it was three o'clock in the afternoon when I was on the wrong side of the volcano. Then I realized that six o'clock East Coast time is actually three o'clock West Coast time!

I was actually struggling for about one hour, trying to get across the wide spot, and Dad was in intercession for one hour. I believe the Lord gave me a "word of wisdom" to use the eight-inch stick to assist me in this struggle. I credit Dad's prayers, which provided God's strength and prevented a dangerous situation from developing.

DANIEL AND THE ANGEL

Scholars believe that the Hebrew prophet Daniel was merely a teenager when he was carried captive into Babylon. Daniel and his Hebrew companions were so in tune with God through prayer that when Daniel was thrown to the lions, the Lord prevented the wild beasts from devouring the man of God. An angel of the Lord spared Daniel's life as he "shut the lions' mouths" (Dan. 6:22). When Daniel's three companions were cast into a fiery furnace, they too were spared from the violence of the flames by a supernatural being, identified as the fourth man, whose appearance was like the Son of God (Dan. 3:25). Angels were quite active on behalf of the Hebrew people during their seventy years of captivity in Babylon.

Eventually Daniel became an old man and was unable to return to Israel with the thousands of Hebrews who departed Babylon to return to their homeland. It was during the time of a political transition when the Medes and Persians overthrew the Babylonians and Daniel remained in power under the new administration.

During this time, Daniel received a prophetic vision related to the time of the end, and was unable to receive the heavenly understanding of this important revelation. He initiated a personal twenty-one-day fast, and after three full weeks, an angel of the Lord appeared to him. The angel revealed that on the first day Daniel had prayed for understanding, God had heard his prayer, but a powerful evil spirit, called the "prince of the kingdom of Persia" (Dan. 10:13), had restrained the angel of the Lord from proceeding to Babylon and revealing to Daniel the insight concerning the vision. Thus, there was a battle in the second heaven between an angel of the Lord and a prince spirit of Satan (Eph. 6:12).

Years ago, while studying this event in Daniel 10, I wondered why, as a young man, Daniel and his companions were able to pray and within twenty-four hours angelic messengers intervened on their behalf, yet when Daniel was older, it appeared there was a more intense struggle in the atmospheric heaven over Babylon. After exploring the Scripture and studying the history at that time, I suggest three possibilities as to why the prayers were hindered.

First, the prayer base had dwindled. After Darius and Cyrus overthrew the king of Babylon, the Jews were permitted by a decree to return to Israel. Ezra chapter 2 lists the names and numbers of those Jews who returned from Babylonian captivity and reveals that 42,360 came out of Babylon and returned to Israel (Ezra 2:64). This departure of godly people would be similar to a mass exodus from a megachurch that runs 15,000 and suddenly loses 14,500. The prayer base would be affected. There is power in unity and strength in numbers, as "one [can] chase a thousand, and two [can] put ten thousand to flight" (Deut. 32:30). When spiritual warfare increases, there must be an increase in the prayer support. Our ministry has a large prayer base called "The Daughters of Rachel" with fifteen hundred women intercessors who continually pray for our ministry and us. Many large ministries made the mistake as they grow larger of concentrating on the business and activity of the ministry and not building a strong foundation of prayer that forms pillars of strength to hold up the building.

Second, Daniel was now much older, possibly in his nineties. A younger person has more strength than an older one.

When David was a young teenager, he was always running. He ran from his carriage to the army, ran toward the army to meet the Philistine, and ran to cut off Goliath's head (1 Sam. 10:23; 17:22, 48). David fought many battles, and in the latter part of his life (after age fifty) he engaged another giant in battle, during which David came near death from a new sword of his enemy (2 Sam. 21:16). He ran into the battle as a teen and nearly ran from the battle in his latter years. Daniel was aged, and the twenty-one-day fast left him completely weak (Dan. 10:8). My own father is seventy-six years of age and has told me that because his physical body is quite worn, it becomes difficult at times to engage in long prayers the way he could when he was younger.

Third, there had been a change in the government of Babylon. Paul wrote that we wrestle not against flesh and blood but against "principalities," which are strong spirits that control nations. Daniel was told there was a "prince of Persia" hindering the answer to his prayer, and the angel revealed that in the future another prince, called the "prince of Greece," would come (Dan. 10:13, 20). These were satanic spirits that dominated the atmosphere over both Persia and Greece and would engage in spiritual wars related to the Persian and Grecian empires. Whenever there is a major change in the leadership of a government, there is often a transition in the spiritual powers that control the atmosphere of that region of the world. Even during the temptation of Christ, Satan offered Jesus the kingdoms of the world if He would worship him. Satan said, "This has been delivered to me, and I give it to whomever I wish" (Luke 4:6). The Medes and Persians over-threw Babylon in one night and introduced a new spiritual power in the atmosphere over Babylon. No doubt, Daniel was battling the spiritual powers overshadowing the atmosphere over the city.

Please note, however, that God sent an angel of the Lord to Daniel after his three-week fast! Once again, we see the ministry of angels released in the lives of those who know and practice the power of prayer and intercession. The power of intercession lies not just in the fact that God hears our prayers but also in the fact that distance is insignificant when it comes to prayer. Not only do our prayers leave Earth and reach vertically upward to heaven, but our prayers also have a horizontal effect as the Lord answers us and stretches His arms around the earth to find the one person for whom we are praying!

A FINAL WORD

In this book you've discovered the supernatural power of the little-known Mizpah covenant to establish the *gate of heaven* in your family's life—just as it did in Jacob's, which will enable God's angels to ascend and descend from heaven as they provide protection to your family. The angel of the Lord kept watch over Jacob and his family, and over the children of Israel as they left the bondage of Egypt and took their forty-year journey to the Promised Land that God had give to them.

The angel of the Lord has kept watch over the children of God throughout the years since Bible times. God's angels are on assignment from God Himself, and as you walk humbly and obediently before your God, His angels will protect and defend you and your family members. Christ Himself stands before our heavenly Father to intercede on your behalf as the Holy Spirit comes alongside to comfort you and to pray through you, even when you are uncertain of what to pray for. You and your precious family are in good hands! Remember that God Himself has given you access to His angels through your diligent fasting and praying. Fasting forms a supernatural hedge of protection around you and your family, and your prayers activate the angels as guardians of your home. The power of your intercession overcomes the barriers of distance, and the angels hear your call and rush to your assistance.

Establish this remarkable covenant in your life today, and begin to experience the blessings of a covenant relationship with God.

Notes

CHAPTER 4
MIZPAH AND THE ANGEL OF THE COVENANT

1. Online PDF version of *Book of Jasher* (Salt Lake City, UT: J. H. Parry & Sons, 1887), http://www.dubroom.org/download/pdf/ebooks/the_book_of_jasher.pdf (accessed January 30, 2009).

CHAPTER 9
ANGELS AND THE MIZPAH COVENANT

1. Perry Stone Jr., *Putting On Your God Gear* (Cleveland, TN: Voice of Evangelism, 2007), 73–75.

CHAPTER 10
THE COVENANT OVER THE THRESHOLD

1. "Inanna," *Encyclopedia Mythica* from Encyclopedia Mythica Online, http://www.pantheon.org/articles/i/inanna.html (accessed March 27, 2009).

2. "Nergal: Lord of the Underworld," http://www.gatewaystobabylon.com/gods/lords/undernergal.html (accessed February 19, 2009).

3. "Sin—Moon God in 2100 B.C.," http://www.bible.ca/islam/islam-photos-moon-worship-archealolgy.htm (accessed February 19, 2009).

4. Josephus, *Antiquities of the Jews*, book 1, chapter 19.

CHAPTER 12
THE MIRACLE OF LONG-DISTANCE INTERCESSION

1. W. E. Vine, *Vine's Expository Dictionary of New Testament Words* (Nashville, TN: Thomas Nelson, 1997), 216.

2. Ibid., 200.

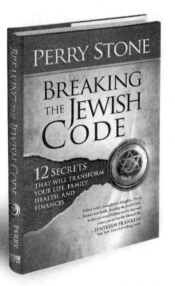

FREE NEWSLETTERS
TO HELP EMPOWER YOUR LIFE

Why subscribe today?

☐ **DELIVERED DIRECTLY TO YOU.** All you have to do is open your inbox and read.

☐ **EXCLUSIVE CONTENT.** We cover the news overlooked by the mainstream press.

☐ **STAY CURRENT.** Find the latest court rulings, revivals, and cultural trends.

☐ **UPDATE OTHERS.** Easy to forward to friends and family with the click of your mouse.

CHOOSE THE E-NEWSLETTER THAT INTERESTS YOU MOST:

- Christian news
- Daily devotionals
- Spiritual empowerment
- And much, much more

SIGN UP AT: **http://freenewsletters.charismamag.com**